Ralph + ... Smith

YOU DONE GOOD
THE JOLLEYS

Thanks for
Everything, the
Robinsons ☺

Grace + York Bayer

The Kenn...
Todd, Lorrai... & boys

R.J. Dalley
Tricia Dalley
Norman Grange

Love ya!

La Dona Smith

D. Goodge

Art & Shirley Ulibarri

Thanks!

Love, Kathe Foutz

Best Wishes
Nedra Shumway & family

Rose J. Washburn

The Clarks

Love,
Dennis, Cheryl Carpenter
and family

Keith & Venice Jackson

Love Ya Lots,

The Reynolds Family

We love you
The Grahams

Bill Graham

Love, Kim
the Stradling family

Mike + Jeri Neal

Del & Becci Talley

Best to you

John + Marge Billingsley

Thanks for Everything
Jed, Holly & Eli
Foutz

Doug—

you are so special

Thank you for all

your time & effort

on our behalf—

Jack & Chris Cook

Ed Slagle

JESUS CHRIST, KEY TO THE PLAN OF SALVATION

Gerald N. Lund

Deseret Book Company
Salt Lake City, Utah

Library of Congress Cataloging-in-Publication Data

Lund, Gerald N.
Jesus Christ, key to the plan of salvation / by Gerald N. Lund.
p. cm.
Includes index.
ISBN 0-87579-421-1
1. Jesus Christ—Mormon interpretations. 2. Salvation. 3. Mormon Church—Doctrines. 4. Church of Jesus Christ of Latter-day Saints—Doctrines. I. Title.
BX8643.J4L85 1991
232′.3—dc20 90-48801
CIP

Printed in the United States of America

10 9 8 7 6 5 4 3 2 1

Contents

Acknowledgments

Chapters 2, 4–6, 8, 10–13 have been adapted from the following articles:

"Do the scriptures give any indication as to what happened to the family of Jesus after his death and resurrection?" September 1975, *Ensign* © The Church of Jesus Christ of Latter-day Saints. Used by permission.

"An Exploration of the Process of Faith As Taught in the Book of Mormon," in *The Second Annual Church Educational System Religious Educators' Symposium: A Symposium on the Book of Mormon, August 17–19, 1978* © The Church of Jesus Christ of Latter-day Saints. Used by permission.

"Old Testament Types and Symbols," in *The Third Annual Church Educational System Religious Educators' Symposium: A Symposium on the Old Testament, August 16–18, 1979* © The Church of Jesus Christ of Latter-day Saints. Used by permission.

"Salvation: By Grace or by Works?" April 1981, *Ensign* © The Church of Jesus Christ of Latter-day Saints. Used by permision.

"To This End Was I Born," in *A Symposium on the New*

Testament, 1984 © The Church of Jesus Christ of Latter-day Saints. Used by permission.

"The Savior said that we should be perfect, even as he and our Father in Heaven are perfect. (See 3 Ne. 12:48.) Are we expected to achieve perfection in this life? If so, how can I avoid becoming discouraged with myself as I try to achieve it?" August 1986, *Ensign* © The Church of Jesus Christ of Latter-day Saints. Used by permission.

"Reflections on the Christmas Story," in *A Celebration of Christmas* © 1988 Deseret Book Company.

"The Fall of Man and His Redemption," in *The Book of Mormon: Second Nephi, the Doctrinal Structure* © 1989 Religious Studies Center, Brigham Young University. Used by permission.

"Divine Indebtedness and the Atonement," in *The Book of Mormon: The Book of Mosiah, Salvation Only through Christ* © 1990 Religious Studies Center, Brigham Young University. Used by permission.

Chapter 1

"No Other Name"

(Mosiah 3:17)

"Wherefore, *thou shalt do all that thou doest in the name of the Son,* and thou shalt repent and call upon God in the name of the Son forevermore." (Moses 5:8; italics added.) So spoke the angel to Adam at the beginning of the world's history. And thus spoke the Lord through the Prophet Joseph Smith in our dispensation: "And again, I say unto you, *all things must be done in the name of Christ.*" (D&C 46:31; italics added.)

From the foundation of the world to the present day, our Lord and Savior Jesus Christ has been the central figure in the plan of the Father to bring to pass the immortality and eternal life of man:

He it was who stepped forward in the Great Council in heaven and offered his life as ransom for all. (See Moses 4: 1–2.)

He it was who, under the direction of the Father, created worlds without number. (See Moses 1:32–33.)

He it was who directed men as Jehovah, God of the Old Testament, for the first four thousand years of this world's history. (See, for example, Abr. 2:6–8.)

He it was who put aside his godly glory, thinking it not

unseemly to take upon himself the frail and corruptible body of mortality. (See Philip. 2:6–8.)

He it was who sweat blood for us in a garden of olive trees; who endured mockery and cruel jibes; who stood with spittle running down his face; who endured the lacerating pain of a Roman scourging and the unspeakable horror of death by crucifixion—all that he might save us from the results of our foolishness and rebellion. (See Luke 22:44; Mark 14:65; 15:29–32; 1 Ne. 19:9.)

He it is who will overthrow Babylon and make the kingdoms of the world become the kingdoms of our God and his Christ. (See Rev. 11:15.)

He it is who will come again in such resplendent glory that the mountains will flow down at his presence and the sun will hide its face in shame. (See D&C 133:44, 49.)

It is little wonder then that Nephi proclaimed, "We talk of Christ, we rejoice in Christ, we preach of Christ, we prophesy of Christ, and we write according to our prophecies, that our children may know to what source they may look for a remission of their sins." (2 Ne. 25:26.)

If one were to count all the times the various names and titles of Jesus are used in scripture—Lord, Savior, Redeemer, Messiah, God, the Lamb, Jesus, Alpha and Omega, the Son of Man, Christ, Master, and dozens more—the total would approach some twenty-five thousand usages in the four standard works. That averages about *ten uses per page of scripture!* Surely that says something about the central role he plays in our lives and in the destiny of all mankind.

For over a quarter of a century, I have had the opportunity to serve in the Church Educational System of The Church of Jesus Christ of Latter-day Saints. As seminary teacher, institute instructor and director, curriculum writer, and administrator, I have been privileged to spend much of my adult life reading, studying, teaching, and writing about the life and mission of the Savior of the world. It has been a labor accompanied by a never-ending and ever-growing sense of awe at the majesty and perfections of the Son of Man. I understand now with much greater clarity the Master's statement when he said, "My yoke is easy, and my burden is light." (Matt. 11:30.)

This work is made up of articles, talks, and teaching aids given over the past few years in various settings and is adapted to focus on Jesus Christ and his place in the plan of salvation. Each piece in its own way was and is meant to bear witness of the Son of God and of the great plan of the Father. My sincere hope is that they bring greater understanding to you and strengthen your own testimony of Jesus Christ and your desire to be more like him and our Heavenly Father. My own testimony is, as King Benjamin said it so well 2,100 years ago, "there shall be no other name given nor any other way nor means whereby salvation can come unto the children of men, *only in and through the name of Christ,* the Lord Omnipotent." (Mosiah 3:17; italics added.)

Chapter 2

"The Birth of Jesus Christ Was on This Wise"

(Matthew 1:18)

"And in the sixth month the angel Gabriel was sent from God unto a city of Galilee, named Nazareth." (Luke 1:26.)

The rabbis of ancient Israel had a saying: "Judea is wheat, Galilee straw, and beyond Jordan, only chaff."[1] The urbane and worldly wise Jerusalemites, privileged to dwell in the Holy City, looked down on all others with condescension; but they especially viewed the Galileans as crude, unlearned, and earthy peasants. For the most part the people of Galilee were men of the soil and of the sea. This kept them in touch with basic values; and in spite of the feelings of the Judeans, they were known for being hard-working and warm-hearted, and for showing unrestrained hospitality and uncompromising honesty.

As for Nazareth itself, like many other villages of Judea and Galilee, it sat amid steep, tree-covered hillsides so as not to utilize precious agricultural land. For a village now so famous to us, it seems to have been of singular insignificance then. It is not even mentioned in the Old Testament or in the extensive writings of the ancient historian Josephus. Nathanael expressed what must have been a common feeling even among the Galileans when he said, "Can there any good thing come out of Nazareth?" (John 1:46.) Evidently, the suggestion that the Messiah had come from such a civic backwater was unthinkable.

But that is not to say that this home village of Mary and Joseph, and later the Master Himself, was a drab and dull setting. One writer describes it as follows: "You cannot see from Nazareth the surrounding country, for Nazareth lies in a basin; but the moment you climb to the edge of the basin . . . what a view you have. Esdraelon lies before you, with its twenty battlefields. . . . There is Naboth's vineyard and the place of Jehu's revenge upon Jezebel; there Shunem and the house of Elisha; the Carmel and the place of Elijah's sacrifice. To the east the valley of Jordan, . . . to the west the radiance of the Great Sea. . . . You can see thirty miles in three directions."[2]

This was the setting in which our story begins.

Engagement of Joseph and Mary

"To a virgin espoused to a man whose name was Joseph, of the house of David." (Luke 1:27.)

As we are dropped into the midst of their lives, Joseph and Mary are "espoused." (Matt. 1:18.) Espousal among the Hebrews was significantly more binding than are our engagements today. The couple entered into it by written agreement and considered it the formal beginning of the marriage itself. While the couple might not actually live together for as much as a year after the betrothal—a time designed to allow the bride to prepare her dowry—the espousal was as legally binding as the formal marriage.

The scriptural text gives no hint of the age of either Mary or Joseph, but from existing sources we can make some educated guesses. We know that puberty began somewhat earlier in the Middle East than is common in Western countries today. Therefore, marriage at earlier ages than we are accustomed to was the general rule. Speaking of men, one rabbi described the stages of development as follows: At five he began study of Torah; at ten, study of the Mishnah (the oral laws); at fifteen, the study of Talmud (the extensive commentaries on the scriptures). *At eighteen,* he married; at twenty, he pursued a trade or business.[3] For a girl, probably the most common age of marriage was fifteen or sixteen. Sometimes it was later, sometimes earlier, but it is likely that Mary was around sixteen and Joseph, her espoused husband, only two or three years older than that.

Nazareth was a small village. Joseph and Mary must have known each other well. How fascinating it would be to know the circumstances that brought them to the point of betrothal. Much is made of the fact that in those days families arranged marriages through the auspices of a matchmaker. No doubt that was true, but that does not mean that the individuals involved had no voice in the matter. We know from contemporary sources that, once the arrangements were made, the consent of the couple was required. The man had a direct say in the choice of his bride, and the woman could refuse the marital arrangements if not to her satisfaction.[4] So what was it that drew these two together?

We know Mary must have been of unusual loveliness. Nephi saw her in vision six hundred years before her birth and described her as "exceedingly fair" and "most beautiful and fair." (1 Ne. 11:13, 15.) But did Joseph see only the outward beauty, or did he sense the same qualities that caused Gabriel to declare that this woman was "highly favoured" of the Lord? (Luke 1:28.) No wonder Joseph loved her! Imagine finding a woman of such remarkable grace and beauty in a small village in the mountains of the Galilee.

And what of Joseph? What was it about this man that caused Mary to give her consent to the marriage arrangements? Only a few scriptural verses tell us about Joseph. He was a carpenter, that we know. (See Matt. 13:55.) And because fathers commonly taught their sons their own trade, Joseph was likely reared in a carpenter's shop at his father's knees. His hands would have been rough and callused. He was a man of labor, a man who created things through his own craftsmanship.

Matthew also describes him as a "just man." (Matt. 1:19.) It is a simple phrase, yet it speaks volumes, for those same words are used to describe men such as Noah, Job, Nephi, and Jacob. Was it purely by accident that such a man was in Nazareth waiting to be Mary's partner in this most significant of dramas? Surely God the Father had seen in Joseph a man worthy to raise His Son and help prepare Him for His mortal ministry. While it would not be Joseph's privilege to actually father the "Firstborn," it would be his labor that would provide for His needs, his voice that would encourage His first steps, his hands that would guide the boy's fingers across the sacred scrolls of the Torah in those first Hebrew lessons. Joseph was also the one who would put a mallet and chisel and plane in those smaller hands so that one day this boy from Nazareth would also be known as "the carpenter." (Mark 6:3.) No wonder Mary loved him!

The Name Mary

"And the virgin's name was Mary." (Luke 1:27.)

One of the most common feminine names in the New Testament is Mary—*Miryam* (Miriam) in Hebrew. One Bible concordance identifies at least seven different Marys in the New Testament, so it is not surprising to find a virgin of that name in the village of Nazareth.[5] But perhaps there is more to it than that. Among Book of Mormon prophets, even a hundred years before the birth of the Savior, the actual name of the woman who was to mother the Messiah was known: It was to be Mary. (See Mosiah 3:8; Alma 7:10.) If that was so among Book of Mormon prophets, is it not possible that the name was also known among Old Testament prophets as well, and therefore among the people of the Holy Land?

We know from existing records that the people at the time of Christ's birth generally believed that the birth of the long-awaited Messiah was imminent. What mother would not hope that her daughter might be the promised vessel for such an honor? Such maternal optimism might explain the frequency with which daughters were named Mary. But for whatever reason, Mary's mother fulfilled prophetic promises when she named her child, little dreaming that her daughter indeed would be the one to do so.

Gabriel's Salutation

"And the angel came in unto her, and said, Hail, thou that art highly favoured, the Lord is with thee: blessed art thou among women. And when she saw him, she was troubled at his saying, and cast in her mind what manner of salutation this should be. And the angel said unto her, Fear not, Mary: for thou hast found favour with God. And, behold, thou shalt conceive in thy womb, and bring forth a son, and shalt call his name Jesus." (Luke 1:28–31.)

It was early July in Galilee.[6] The heat, even at night, can be stifling and oppressive. Luke indicates that Mary and Joseph were likely of poor families.[7] If that be the case, the house of Mary's family would have been small, no more than one or two rooms curtained off for sleeping and privacy at night.

We are not told if it was day or night, or if she was alone in the house; surely she must have felt a sudden clutch of fear when she looked up and saw a personage standing there before her. All of us have had someone come up behind us or appear in a doorway unexpectedly and startle us. We give an involuntary cry of surprise and feel the quick burst of adrenalin that leaves the heart pounding, the palms sweaty, and the mouth dry. So it is not difficult to imagine the shock of having not just a man appear suddenly in your room, but a being of transcendent radiance and glory.

But the shock of Gabriel's sudden appearance could not have been any greater than the stunning impact of his words. First there was the "impossible" announcement that she was about to conceive. Her response is so spontaneous, so logical. It adds even further to the power and simplicity with which Luke tells us of this night. One can almost picture her blurting it out, in spite of the glory of the being standing before her: "How shall this be, seeing I know not a man?" (Luke 1:34.)

But that was only the first of the stunning pronouncements. The Messiah had been foretold for four millennia. Now to realize that the long centuries of waiting had come to an end, that the Messiah was about to be born, and that she—Mary of Nazareth—was to be the mother! Add to that the declaration that, for the first and only time in the history of the world, this was to be a virgin birth, and the revelation was even more staggering. This simple, pure woman from a little-known city in Galilee was to carry in her womb the divine offspring of the great Elohim Himself. Her son would be the Son of God!

Only when we consider the magnitude of those statements do we begin to appreciate how marvelous is Mary's answer. There were no questioning looks, no stammering demands of "Why me?" There were no murmurs of doubt. There was no disputation, no hesitation, no wondering. She simply said, in glorious and touching simplicity: "Behold the handmaid of the Lord; be it unto me according to thy word." (Luke 1:38.)

Mary's Pregnancy

"Now the birth of Jesus Christ was on this wise: When as his mother Mary was espoused to Joseph, before they came together, she was found with child of the Holy Ghost." (Matt. 1:18.)

At the command of Gabriel, Mary left Nazareth to visit her cousin Elizabeth, wife of Zacharias the priest, living in Judea. Elizabeth was six months pregnant with a miracle of her own, and Mary abode with her kinswoman about three months until the time came for Elizabeth to deliver.

Consider for a moment what coming back to Nazareth at that point must have meant for Mary. She suddenly, unexpectedly departed from her home for an extended stay far to the south. When she returned, the growing within the womb was pushing outward, expanding now to swell the mother's belly. It is not a secret that can be hidden for long.

This was not a society like our own where immorality is not only tolerated but often openly flaunted. Modesty and virtue were deeply ingrained into the fiber of the nation and were especially strong in the small towns and villages of Israel. Imagine the effect on that tiny village when Mary returned and the first of the village women began to notice the change in her.

Anyone who has ever lived in the tightly knit, closely bonded society of a small town or village can predict with some accuracy what happened next. At first there would have been only questioning looks and quick shakings of the heads. Surely such could not be so. Not Mary. Perhaps she was just putting on a little weight. Then more and more voices would have questioned, not openly, of course, but in whispers, at the well each day as they came together for water, or while doing the laundry on the banks of a stream.

Was Mary allowed to tell others of her visit from Gabriel? Matthew's comment, "she was *found* with child," would imply not. (Italics added.) But even if she were allowed to tell, would such a "wildly fantastic" claim have quelled the rumors? A virgin birth? Mother of the Messiah? A child fathered by God Himself? Either she was mad or took them for absolute fools to imagine they would believe such a story. To the villagers, her departure from the village "with haste" took on new and ominous significance. (See Luke 1:39.) And poor Joseph. Victim of such "infidelity." What would he do now?

Joseph Takes Mary to Wife

"Then Joseph her husband, being a just man, and not willing to make her a publick example, was minded to put her away privily. But while he thought on these things, behold, the angel of the Lord appeared unto him in a dream, saying, Joseph, thou son of David, fear not to take unto thee Mary thy wife: for that which is conceived in her is of the Holy Ghost. . . . Then Joseph being raised from sleep did as the angel of the Lord had bidden him, and took unto him his wife." (Matt. 1:19–20, 24.)

Neither Luke nor Matthew gives us much detail, but we can read the pain and embarrassment between the lines. Here was a good man, faithful in every respect. What pain must have filled his soul to learn that his betrothed was with child! Surely not Mary, not his lovely and chaste Mary. We can only guess at the agony of spirit he must have experienced at the confirmation of her "unfaithfulness."

How many men would let the bitterness and anger of such betrayal fester and boil over into a blind desire for revenge that can cause people to strike out, seeking to hurt as deeply as they themselves are hurt? By Mosaic law, adultery was punishable by death. (See, for example, John 8:5; Lev. 20:10.) Joseph could have taken Mary to the elders of the village and demanded justice. But, despite the pain he must have felt, despite the personal humiliation, he would not put his beloved Mary through the shame and danger of a public trial. He would simply dissolve the marriage contract quietly.

But then again, in one blinding instant of revelation, all was explained and put right. In response to Gabriel's incredible announcement, Mary had simply said, "Behold the handmaid of the Lord." Now Joseph heard the same stunning pronouncement. We gain a glimpse of the greatness of the man from his response. Matthew says it in one phrase: "Then Joseph *being raised from sleep* . . . took unto him his wife." (Matt. 1:24; italics added.) The verse suggests that little time elapsed between the announcement and the marriage, perhaps even occurring entirely before dawn.

As with Mary, Joseph accepted without question the fantastic nature of the declaration. There was no vacillation. Surely he knew his fellow villagers well enough to know that a hasty marriage in the middle of the night would only fuel the rumors. All he would accomplish by such an action would be to bring the onus of doubt and shame upon himself. But the angel had spoken. His doubts were resolved. His Mary had been proven faithful. And so he arose from his bed and took her to be his wife.

The Town Called Bethlehem

"And it came to pass in those days, that there went out a decree from Caesar Augustus, that all the world should be taxed. . . . And all went to be taxed, every one into his own city. And Joseph also went up from Galilee, out of the city of Nazareth, unto Judaea, unto the city of David, which is called Bethlehem; (because he was of the house and lineage of David:) to be taxed with Mary his espoused wife, being great with child." (Luke 2:1, 3–5.)

Bethlehem. The city of David. Ancient homeland of Israel's greatest king. In Hebrew it is called *Beth Lechem*. Literally, *Beth Lechem* means "The House of Bread."[8] How perfect that He who was to take the throne of David and become

Israel's ultimate king should come to earth in the city of His illustrious ancestor! How fitting that He who would be known as the "Bread of Life" should enter mortality in the tiny village called "The House of Bread." (See John 6:35.)

Though His birth is celebrated in December, latter-day revelation explains that it actually occurred in the spring.[9] (See D&C 20:1.) The time would have been late March or early April when Joseph moved southward with Mary at his side, heavy with the living treasure in her womb. Spring is a time of glorious beauty in Israel. The "latter rains" water the parched soil, and in gratitude the earth responds with an explosion of grass and wildflowers. New life springs from the old with the wildest abundance. What better season to welcome him who would be called the "Prince of Life"? (See Acts 3:15.)

Search for Lodgings

"And so it was, that, while they were there, the days were accomplished that she should be delivered. And she brought forth her firstborn son, and wrapped him in swaddling clothes, and laid him in a manger; because there was no room for them in the inn." (Luke 2:6–7.)

No room in the inn. If, as we believe, it was April and not December, then it was very likely Passover season in Jerusalem. This could explain the reason Joseph took Mary on the rigorous, sixty-mile journey to Judea when she was in the final month of her pregnancy. The Roman "taxing" mentioned by Luke was more accurately a census or enrollment. Each family head had to register and give an accounting of their property so that taxes could be levied. But while there was considerable flexibility in timing allowed to meet this requirement, if it was Passover season, that would allow them to meet two responsibilities. The Mosaic Law required that every adult male bring his sacrifices before the Lord (i.e., to the temple) each year at Passover. (See Ex. 23:14–19.) So by choosing this time of year, Joseph could fulfill both requirements.

Today we can hardly conceive of the magnitude of this most important of all Jewish festivals. From all over the empire, Jews returned to their homeland at Passover. Though determining exactly how large Jerusalem was during this period is difficult, a fairly accurate guess would place the population between one and two hundred thousand. Josephus tells us that during Passover "innumerable multitudes came thither [to Jerusalem] out of the country."[10] In another place, he was even more specific. Because the Paschal lamb had to be totally consumed by the family in the ritual meal, tradition stated that no fewer than ten and no more than twenty could gather for each lamb sacrificed. (See Ex. 12:10.) Josephus tells us that during one Passover of his time (about A.D. 70), 256,500 lambs were sacrificed.[11] Even using the more conservative figure of ten, that still means the population of Jerusalem at Passover had swollen by more than 1000 percent to the staggering number of nearly three million people.

The throngs must have been incredible, the facilities throughout the city taxed beyond belief. And with Bethlehem only six miles south of Jerusalem, no wonder there was no room at the inn. Luke probably could have said with equal accuracy, "There was no room anywhere."

Often in the art and literature surrounding the Christmas story, the unknown, unnamed innkeeper of the scriptural account is viewed as selfish and uncaring, an insensitive oaf unmoved by the plight of a woman heavy with child. This may make for interesting art and literature, but it is not justified by the scriptural record. In the first place, the "inns" of the Middle East were not quaint and homey little buildings with thatched roofs and latticed windows from which warm lamplight beckoned the weary traveler. The inns of the Holy

Land were typically large, fortress-like buildings, built around a spacious open square. Called *khans* or *caravanserai,* they provided stopping places for the caravans of the ancient world.

Just as modern hotels and motels must provide parking for automobiles, so did a *caravanserai* have to provide a place where the donkeys, camels, and other animals could be safely cared for. Inside the *khan,* which was usually of two-story construction, all the "rooms" faced the courtyard. They were typically arched, open antechambers facing out onto the square. Here the traveler could build a small fire or sleep within clear view of his animals and goods. "In these hostelries, bazaars and markets were held, animals killed and meat sold, also wine and cider; so that they were a much more public place of resort than might at first be imagined."[12]

Even if there had been room at the inn, a *caravanserai* was hardly the ideal place for a woman in labor. Perhaps the innkeeper, moved with compassion at Mary's plight and knowing of her need and desire for privacy, offered them his stable. Perhaps Joseph found the place on his own. The scriptures do not say. But one thing is very probable, and this contradicts another popular misconception. The birth likely did not take place in a wooden shed with pitched roof as is so commonly depicted in nativity scenes around the world.

In Bethlehem today stands the Church of the Nativity. Beneath the church is a large grotto or cave. In southern Judea, including the area around Bethlehem, limestone caves are common. Such caves provided natural shelter for the flocks and herds of ancient Israel. They were warm, safe from inclement weather, and could easily be blocked to keep the animals safe for the night. The tradition that this grotto was the stable of Luke's account is very old and accepted by many scholars. President Harold B. Lee, then of the Council of the

Twelve, visited this grotto in 1958 and confirmed that in his mind it was "a hallowed spot, . . . a sacred place."[13]

So there in the sheltered warmth of the cave, beneath the limestone hills of Bethlehem, He who was to become the Good Shepherd—not of the sheep that grazed the hills of Israel, but of the human flock—was born and cradled in a manger.

That seems almost beyond our comprehension. Here was Jesus—a member of the Godhead, the Firstborn of the Father, the Creator, Jehovah of the Old Testament—now leaving His divine and holy station; divesting Himself of all that glory and majesty and entering the body of a tiny infant; helpless, completely dependent on His mother and earthly father. That He should not come to the finest of earthly palaces and be swaddled in purple and showered with jewels but should come to a lowly stable is astonishing. Little wonder that the angel should say to Nephi, "Behold the condescension of God!" (1 Ne. 11:26.)

Announcement to the Shepherds

"And there were in the same country shepherds abiding in the field, keeping watch over their flock by night. And, lo, the angel of the Lord came upon them, and the glory of the Lord shone round about them: and they were sore afraid. And the angel said unto them, Fear not: for, behold, I bring you good tidings of great joy, which shall be to all people. For unto you is born this day in the city of David a Saviour, which is Christ the Lord. And this shall be a sign unto you; Ye shall find the babe wrapped in swaddling clothes, lying in a manger." (Luke 2:8–12.)

One of these verses is frequently misquoted: "Keeping watch over their *flocks* by night." But the verse does not say *flocks,* plural, but *flock,* singular. One scholar explained the significance: "There was near Bethlehem, on the road to Jerusalem, a tower known as *Migdal Eder,* or *the watchtower of the flock.* Here was the station where shepherds watched the flocks destined for sacrifice in the temple. . . . It was a settled conviction among the Jews that the Messiah was to be born in Bethlehem, and equally that he was to be revealed from Migdal Eder. The beautiful significance of the revelation of the infant Christ to shepherds watching the flocks destined for sacrifice needs no comment."[14] The flock mentioned in the scripture, then, apparently was the one used for temple sacrifices, and the shepherds thus had responsibility for the most important flock in the region.

Sometimes in translation the power of the original language is considerably lessened. While the words, in English, of the angel to the shepherds are beautiful and significant, we miss much of the electrifying impact the original words must have had on those men of Judea. Let us just examine two or three of the phrases as we assume they were given in Aramaic to the shepherds that night.

"In the city of David." We have already seen that the Jews expected Bethlehem to be the birthplace of the Messiah. This in part stemmed directly from the prophet Micah, who centuries before had specified the place. (See Micah 5:2.)

"Is born a Savior." The word that meant "Savior" was *Yeshua.* In the Greek New Testament that name was transliterated into *Hee-ay-sous,* or, in English, "Jesus." When the angel announced to Joseph that Mary would bear a son, note what he said: "Thou shalt call his name Jesus [*Yeshua*]: for he shall *save* the people from their sins." (Matt. 1:21, italics added.)

"Which is Christ." Our English word *Christ* is derived directly from the Greek, *Christos.* It means "the anointed one."[15] *Christos* was a direct translation of the Hebrew word, *Messhiach,* which meant exactly the same thing—the anointed one. *Messhiach* is of course transliterated into English as "Messiah."

"The Lord." The simple title, "Lord," is perhaps the most significant of all, yet we totally miss its importance in the translation. In the Old Testament the name of God was written with four Hebrew consonants: YHVH. Because they did not write vowels, there has been some debate as to its proper pronunciation. Modern scholars often write it as YAHVEH, but the King James translators wrote it as JEHOVAH.

The Jews of ancient times, however, viewed the name as being so sacred that it should not be pronounced out loud. Whenever they found it written, they would substitute the Hebrew word *Adonai,* meaning the Lord. The translators who produced the King James Version of the Old Testament honored that tradition of the Jews, and where they found the name YHVH, they wrote in (with very few exceptions) "the Lord." However, *adonai* can also be used as a title of respect for men, such as in the phrase, "My lord, the king." To distinguish between the two uses, the translators wrote *Lord* in small capital letters if it represented the name of deity, and regular upper and lower case letters if used normally. (See, for example, 2 Sam. 15:21, where both uses are found in the same verse.) The declaration of the angel to the shepherds obviously used *Lord* or *Adonai* in reference to deity; literally it could be translated *Jehovah.*

Now we begin to sense the impact of the angel's words upon these shepherds. In essence, here is his pronouncement: "Unto you is born this day in the city prophesied to be the birthplace of the Messiah, *Yeshua* [or Jesus], the Savior, who is the Anointed One (the Messiah), and who is also Jehovah, the God of your fathers."

"And they came with haste, and found Mary, and Joseph, and the babe lying in a manger. And when they had seen it, they made known abroad the saying which was told them concerning this child. And all they that heard it wondered at those things which were told them by the shepherds. But Mary kept all these things, and pondered them in her heart." (Luke 2:16–19.)

Chapter 3

"He Hath Anointed Me to Preach the Gospel to the Poor"

(Luke 4:18)

One time at lunch, a friend raised an interesting question: Suppose the Savior were to visit your ward this Sunday, where would he go first? There were several of us at the table, but we all agreed that he might stop first at the bishop's office and say something like "I thought I'd let you know I'm here. I'll be back to see you in a while." Then he'd go to the nursery, where he would kneel, and the children would gather around him. Then we decided he would go next to the Primary.

From there we weren't sure where he would go. Someone said, "I think I know what he'd do next," and he cited a scripture in the Book of Luke, chapter four. As the chapter number indicates, the Savior's ministry had just begun. In fact, the beginning parts of chapter four are the temptations of Jesus. Verse thirteen relates that, after the devil had ended all the temptations, Satan departed from the Lord for a season, and verse fourteen says that Jesus returned in the power of the Spirit into Galilee. That is the setting.

In the Synagogue

Verse sixteen begins the scene: *"And he came to Nazareth, where he had been brought up: and, as his custom was, he went into the synagogue on the sabbath day."* The phrase "as his custom was" reveals quite a bit about the Lord's habits and priorities. As important as the Savior's word was, and as many people as were demanding to be with him, every sabbath day he was in the synagogue where he should have been.

"And stood up for to read." The Jewish practice was for all the people in the synagogue to sit on benches. However, they never sat to read the scriptures—they stood. The great scroll of the scriptures was opened, and various members of the synagogue would come up and read from the scriptures. Thus the Savior stood to take that privilege.

"And there was delivered unto him the book of the prophet Esaias [or Isaiah]. And when he had opened the book, he found the place where it was written." (V. 17.) That last phrase suggests that Jesus went specifically to a scripture that he wanted to read, rather than just choosing a verse at random.

This is what he read from Isaiah on the scroll: *"The Spirit of the Lord is upon me, because he hath anointed me to preach the gospel to the poor; he hath sent me to heal the brokenhearted, to preach deliverance to the captives, and recovering of sight to the blind, to set at liberty them that are bruised, to preach the acceptable year of the Lord."* (Vv. 18–19.)

The Messiah *"closed the book, and he gave it again to the minister, and sat down. And the eyes of all them that were in the synagogue were fastened on him. And he began to say unto them, This day is this scripture fulfilled in your ears."* (Vv. 20–21.) The implication was obvious—Jesus Christ was suggesting, I am the fulfillment of what I just read.

The Lord's Ministry

The man in our lunch group who referred to those verses in Luke said, "I think that after the Savior visited the Primary, he would return to the bishop and ask, 'Do you have anyone in your ward with a special need? Do you have anyone who is in particular stress right now? Have you anyone who is deeply sorrowful? I would like to visit them. Then I'll come back and talk with you and other members of the ward to see what other needs you have.' " I too think that is what the Savior would do because that is what he said his calling was.

What, then, was the Savior's ministry, as Isaiah defined it and the Savior announced it? Notice what verse eighteen says, *"The Spirit of the Lord is upon me,* because *he hath anointed me to preach the gospel to the poor."* (Emphasis added.) The one word *because* may seem unusual here. The Lord didn't say the Spirit of the Lord is upon me, *therefore* I will teach the gospel to the poor. Nor did he say the Spirit of the Lord is upon me *so that* I can preach the gospel. He said the Spirit of the Lord is upon me *because* I have been anointed to preach to the poor. Perhaps I am reading more into the word than is actually there, but as I read it, I think the Lord was saying *because* of the challenges inherent in what I have been called to do—to preach to the poor, to reach the broken-hearted, and so on—*because* of that, I have the Spirit. In other words, success in fulfilling those needs necessitates having the Spirit.

The entire phrase, *"because he hath anointed me,"* is also significant. In Greek the verb for anoint is *chrio,* from which comes from the word *Christos* or, in English, Christ. In Hebrew the verb for anoint is *mashack,* from which comes the Hebrew title *Messhiach* or, in English, Messiah. The titles

Christ or Messiah thus mean "the anointed one." So when the Savior said, "he has anointed me," he was identifying himself as the anointed one, the long-awaited Messiah, the Christ. It was very clearly an announcement of who he was.

Isaiah succinctly describes what the Messiah would be anointed to do: *"to preach the gospel to the poor."* In Greek, two different words for *poor people* are used in the New Testament. One means specifically a person who earns a very meager or scanty wage. The other means someone who is totally destitute. The second word is often applied to beggars because they earn no wage and therefore have to live upon the alms of others. Interestingly, Luke here used the latter word, so that Jesus was saying, "The Lord has anointed me to preach the gospel to those who are totally destitute." Those who are beggars spiritually, who basically have no resources are the ones the Savior is to provide resources for. (Compare with King Benjamin's reminder in Mosiah 4:19–20 that we are all beggars before God.)

The next phrase, *"he hath sent me to heal the brokenhearted,"* is especially full of hope. How many broken hearts are there in the world? How many of us are sorrowing, suffering from difficult circumstances or challenges? The Lord was sent to heal such people — to make whole those hearts that have been rent asunder.

The word *captive* in the next phrase, *"to preach deliverance to the captives,"* is also a bit peculiar. In Greek it is a combination of two words meaning those who are taken at spear point. So a captive is not just a prisoner, but a prisoner of war. What an apt description. How many prisoners of the great war that started in the premortal existence and continues to our day do we see before us? Appropriately, Nephi spoke of "the captivity of the devil" — it is Satan who takes captive those who have delivered themselves over "to the hardness of their hearts and the blindness of their minds." (1 Ne. 14:7.)

Appropriately, such captives are delivered not through mighty power, but through preaching. They have enslaved themselves, and hearing the truth and accepting it can free them. Did not the Lord also say, "Ye shall know the truth, and the truth shall make you free." (John 8:32.) Jesus said he was sent to preach deliverance. The word *preach* implies so much more than simply teaching, because preaching in the New Testament involves declaring and bearing testimony of God's word so that the Spirit can validate that testimony as truthful.

The next phrase, *"and recovering of sight to the blind,"* also contains a highly significant word. Jesus did not talk about *giving* sight to the blind, but about *recovering* sight to the blind. These are people who once saw but now are blinded. I suspect that the blinding could come from many kinds of darkness—sin, guilt, shame, low self-esteem, ignorance, and so on. It doesn't really matter what the cause of darkness is if a person cannot see. But in all cases Christ provides the illumination to help us see again.

The final phrase, *"to set at liberty them that are bruised,"* in Greek means literally those who are broken to pieces, those who are battered. The Lord does more than heal broken-hearted people. His mission is to free from abuse those who are battered. This is a great message of hope to those who see no way out from misery.

The Jubilee Year

In verse nineteen, the Lord declared that he was come *"to preach the acceptable year of the Lord."* That is a difficult phrase because we're not exactly sure what the acceptable year of the Lord is. An alternate translation of the phrase is "to preach the year of the Lord's favor." Thus many biblical scholars feel that the phrase alludes to the jubilee year of the Old Testament, which is the most holy year the Lord has decreed and thus the most favorable, or acceptable, to him. Leviticus 25:8 explains how often a jubilee year was to occur: "Thou shalt number seven sabbaths of years unto thee, seven times seven years; and the space of the seven sabbaths of years shall be unto thee forty and nine years." So every fiftieth year came to be called the jubilee year (from verse eleven: "A jubile shall that fiftieth year be unto you.")

The jubilee year was a special sabbatical year. Every seventh year, the land was to rest—nothing could be planted, cultivated, or pruned. People were to eat only what grew of itself and then only what they needed at the time. (See Lev. 25:1–7.) The Lord promised that the year before, the sixth year, the land would bear three times its normal yield to feed the people during the sabbath year: "If ye shall say, What shall we eat the seventh year? behold, we shall not sow, nor gather in our increase: then I will command my blessing upon you in the sixth year, and it shall bring forth fruit for three years." (Vv. 20–21.)

Verses nine and ten in particular explain some of the unique features of the jubilee year: "Then shalt thou cause the trumpet of the jubile to sound on the tenth day of the seventh month, in the day of atonement shall ye make the trumpet sound throughout all your land. And ye shall hallow the fiftieth year, and proclaim liberty throughout all the land unto all the inhabitants thereof: . . . ye shall return every man unto his possession, and ye shall return every man unto his family."

Israelites were to set any bond servants free, give any slaves their liberty, and forgive any debtors their debts. What sweeping changes in an economy! Imagine the panic that would be sent into the banking community today to say all debts would be forgiven. Imagine too the consequences of property being returned. If a person, perhaps through foolishness or because of poverty, had sold his inheritance, that family property would be restored to him on the fiftieth year.

Though the meaning of the phrase "to preach the acceptable year of the Lord" may seem obscure to us, the imagery the Lord evoked in the minds of the people who heard him was powerful and sweeping. Its import was "I am here. I have been anointed to proclaim the acceptable year of the Lord. This is a jubilee year: a year when we shall set the captives free, when we shall free the debtors from debt, and when we shall restore them to their inheritances."

Isaiah's Prophecy of the Messiah's Ministry

In the synagogue, the Lord quoted from Isaiah 61:1–2.[1] He did not quote all of Isaiah's prophecy, however, or at least Luke does not record that he quoted all of it. The prophecy in Isaiah that refers to what the Messiah would do continues to the end of verse three. It expands further upon the Lord's ministry. Verse two, for instance, tells us that the Messiah was to also proclaim *"the day of vengeance of our God."* The Lord would preach a spiritual year of jubilee, but at the same time he would proclaim that the day of retribution would fall upon the wicked. Though the world can look to the Savior with great hope, those who refuse to repent and who continue in unrighteousness will have great need to fear the justice of God.

Verses two and three continue with these words about mourning: *"To comfort all that mourn; to appoint unto them that mourn in Zion, to give unto them beauty for ashes, the oil of joy for mourning, the garment of praise for the spirit of heaviness."* While there is no object after the word *appoint,* the implication from the three phrases that follow, which tell what is to be appointed, suggest that gladness will come to those who mourn in Zion. Such sufferers, then, have the promise that the Savior will comfort them and turn their sorrow to joy.

In Old Testament times during periods of deep, deep grief or tragedy, mourners took off the normal clothes and put on sackcloth, which is made from black, woven goat hair five times rougher than burlap. They then took ashes and put them on their heads and on their bodies. This was the sign of mourning, and that is the imagery Isaiah uses here. The Savior will take away the ashes and give them beauty; instead of mourning, there will be the oil of joy.

The Savior will also exchange "the garment of praise for the spirit of heaviness." Think how many of us have the spirit of heaviness. Too often, we may have this spirit not through faulty pride, but through a faulty sense of insecurity, a sense that God is not pleased with us. So we become heavy in our minds and hearts. Instead, the Savior will use a garment of praise for what we are. Compared to the world's criticism, this will be glorious clothing indeed.

I think I learned in a small way what this means. When one of my sons was sixteen, he seemed to have a gift for getting under my skin. One day, after I had asked him many times to close the garage door because the garage had some things in it I didn't want to show up missing, I gritted my teeth and said, "Stephen, let me say something to you." He hunched down, expecting an attack.

Right at that moment, a thought suddenly flashed into my mind: "You're always comparing him to what he ought to be, and he always falls short. But have you ever compared him to what he is and has done?" I thought of a good friend whose sixteen-year-old was in a reform school, and I thought of other sixteen-year-olds I had met whose lives were wrecked. So I said to him, "Are you listening?"

"Yeah, I'm listening," he replied.

I said, "I just want to say to you, thanks for what you

are. I've never had to hassle you about going to Church. You always do your priesthood duties. You didn't date until you were sixteen, and that was your own free will and choice. I've never said this before, and I just thought it was about to time to say, thanks for what you are."

He gave me a long, incredulous look and finally said, "Are you kidding me?" I thought, What a tragedy. He's been criticized so often he doesn't expect praise. Too often we press on our youth the garment of heaviness rather than the garment of praise.

The final image in Isaiah's prophecy is truly beautiful. Isaiah gives the reason why the Savior would do what he does—why he appoints gladness for joy, why he changes mourning into happiness, why he gives praise instead of heaviness. He does it all so that we *"might be called trees of righteousness, the planting of the Lord, that he might be glorified."* His purpose is that we might be as sturdy as trees in our righteousness, cultivated by the Lord; not that we might be glorified but that God might be glorified.

By his own direct revelation in the synagogue at Nazareth, Jesus Christ has told us what his ministry is. And we know, because we are trying to be one with him, that it is a shared ministry with his disciples: "Neither pray I for these alone, but for them also which shall believe on me through their word; that they all may be one; as thou, Father, art in me, and I in thee, that they also may be one in us: that the world may believe that thou hast sent me." (John 17:20–21.)

His purposes are also ours—that we reach out to the poor, that we touch the brokenhearted, that we seek out those who are bruised, that we find those who are laden with heaviness and lighten that heaviness with genuine praise, that we seek those who mourn, whether from family problems, physical impairments, or mental difficulties, it doesn't matter. We seek everyone at the level of his or her needs. We try to show them what the will of the Lord is for them, and then we help them discover how to implement that will in their lives. That is our mission—whether we are General Authorities, teachers of the incarcerated, or neighbors with simple faith. The wonderful hope the Savior offers may be realized by any one of his brothers and sisters, and we may share in that divine work.

Chapter 4

"To This End Was I Born"

(John 18:37)

In the judgment hall of the Antonia Fortress in Jerusalem, two men faced each other in the early hours of a spring morning—the one a man of the world, supreme political ruler of the province of Judea; the other, a Galilean accused of treason, sedition, and blasphemy, who should have been summarily dismissed and sent to the cross. Pilate had done that very thing numerous times before.

But this man—something in his bearing caused the procurator to pause. "Art thou a king then?" he demanded. And the man from Nazareth, facing death in a few hours, responded, "To this end was I born, and for this cause came I into the world, that I should bear witness unto the truth." (John 18:37.)

We cannot possibly argue which portion of Christ's ministry is the most significant, for each aspect of his mission is an integral part of the whole design. It would be safe to say, however, that the events connected with the Last Supper, the Garden of Gethsemane, his arrest and trial, his crucifixion, and his resurrection were the culminating events of his ministry. From the day of his birth and through every step of his ministry, his face was set toward Jerusalem, the cross, and the empty tomb. The following sections are some random thoughts on the events of those last hours of the mortal life of the Master.

Exertion and Exhaustion

Talking about the physical pain and agony of the Crucifixion is a fairly common thing for us, but too often we overlook the fact that the last twenty-four hours of Christ's life must have been physically, emotionally, and mentally exhausting for him. Think back on a time when you had to go for an extended time without sleep. By the time twenty or so sleepless hours have passed, we tend to get mentally sluggish, emotionally irritable, and physically drained. By the time the Savior died on the cross, he had been without sleep for at least thirty-six hours, possibly more. The disciples had unsuccessfully fought off sleep part way into the night (see Matt. 26:40–45), but he went on through that night and all the next day.

Added to the exhaustion caused by lack of sleep was the physical exhaustion caused by pain. Most of us have had an experience with how a very minor pain, such as a toothache or headache, can drain the body's resources. Imagine the drain that accompanied the incomprehensible agony in the Garden, the physical abuse during the trial, and the scourging by the Romans that flayed strips of skin and flesh from his back.

Many of us have given blood to the Red Cross or to a hospital. Remember how physically drained we felt after that experience and of the cautions we were given for rest and nourishment? In the Garden of Gethsemane, Christ suffered so intensely that he bled at *every* pore. (See Luke 22:44; D&C 19:18.) What effect would that loss of blood have had in addition to the physical suffering it caused?

Furthermore, Jesus had to exert himself physically during those last twenty-four hours. He walked from the Upper Room, where he had held the Passover with his disciples, to the Garden of Gethsemane, where he was arrested and taken back to the Palace of Caiaphas. From there he was taken to the Antonia Fortress, then to Herod's Palace, then to the Antonia Fortress again, and finally to Golgotha. That represents nearly five miles of walking up and down some very hilly terrain, and all of it under extreme physical, mental, and emotional duress.

Yet in spite of all of this – no sleep, loss of blood, extensive walking, intense agony, physical abuse – Jesus never once lost his temper, never once lost control of himself or of the situation. In fact, no one could have been more fully composed or in control of himself than was the Master throughout the whole ordeal of his arrest, trial, and crucifixion.

Who Crucified Jesus?

As we review the events of the Savior's arrest, trial, and crucifixion, we should understand who was really responsible for the death of Jesus. Throughout the centuries, Christians have used the accounts of the Crucifixion as justification for their hatred and persecution of the Jews. On the other hand, in more recent times Jewish and Christian leaders who abhor what has happened in the past have tried to put the blame for the Crucifixion solely on the Romans.

A careful reading of the Gospel accounts makes it clear that the primary instigators of the plot to kill the Savior were the Jewish *religious leaders.* They were the ones the Master and his teachings most threatened, and they were the ones who engineered the arrest and the trial before the Sanhedrin and who finally badgered the weak and vacillating Pilate into pronouncing the death sentence. Though Roman hands held the whip and drove the nails, the Roman soldiers were only carrying out the will and careful planning of the Jewish leaders. The Jewish leaders, not the Jewish people as a whole, and not even all of the leaders, were the ones who plotted Jesus' death.

Peter was a Jew. James and John were Jews. Martha, Lazarus, and Zacchaeus—all of the first leaders and disciples of Christianity were Jews. Within a few months of the Crucifixion, over eight thousand people of the Jewish nation had become Christians, including "a great company of the priests." (See Acts 2:41; 4:4; 6:7.) If the Jews as a people are to be blamed for the Crucifixion, then the Jews must equally be given credit for establishing the early Christian church, for Jews as individuals were involved in both.

But doesn't the Book of Mormon prophesy that the Jews would suffer persecution because they crucified Jesus? Not exactly. Some of the Book of Mormon writers did prophesy that the Jews would suffer persecution. The reason for their persecution, however, was not the Crucifixion per se but an attitude of the heart. This distinction is an important one. Nephi said: "As for those who are at Jerusalem, saith the prophet, they shall be scourged by all people, because they crucify the God of Israel, *and turn their hearts aside,* rejecting signs and wonders, and the power and glory of the God of Israel. And because *they turn their hearts aside,* saith the prophet, *and have despised the Holy One of Israel,* they shall wander in the flesh, and perish, and become a hiss and a by-word, and be hated among all nations." (1 Ne. 19:13–14; italics added.)

It is hardness of heart in the Lord's covenant people that brings suffering upon them. It was true of the House of Israel in the Old Testament. It was true of the Nephites and Jaredites in the Book of Mormon. And it was true of some Latter-day Saints in this dispensation. (See, for example, D&C 97:25–27; 101:1–8.)

We believe that punishment for someone else's sin is unjust. (See A of F 1.) To suggest that Jews of the twentieth century are being punished by God for what their ancestors two millennia ago did is unthinkable when we understand God's nature. But those who have been called to be God's people are expected to serve him with all their hearts. (See Deut. 6:5.) When they do not, they bring sorrow and suffering upon themselves.

"None Other Nation . . . Would Crucify Their God"

Another important point has to do with the nature of the Jewish leaders and the conspiracy to kill Jesus. In the Upper Room after he had finished the washing of the feet, Jesus made a rather sobering prophecy—a prophecy that in his own case would be fulfilled in less than twenty-four hours. He said: "If the world hate you, ye know that it hated me before it hated you. If ye were of the world, the world would love his own: but because ye are not of the world, but I have chosen you out of the world, therefore the world hateth you." (John 15:18–19.) And then he added: "These things have I spoken unto you, that ye should not be offended. They shall put you out of the synagogues"—now here is the prophecy—"yea, the time cometh, that whosoever killeth you *will think that he doeth God service.*" (John 16:1–2; italics added.)

The men who killed Jesus were evil men. Criminals killed him—but not criminals in the usual sense. They were criminals motivated by religious motives. H. Curtis Wright shared this important insight on the arrest and crucifixion of Jesus:

> To begin with, the conspiracy against Jesus was *inspired by the religious motives of pious public officials* whose sense of virtue had been outraged. We must disagree violently with the bulk of Christian writers who have described the leaders of the Jews as hoodlums and outlaws, rascals and ruffi-

> ans. . . . They were criminals all right, but of a vastly different piece. They had no use for the seamy side of crime, and they campaigned relentlessly against it. . . . They moved in the upper strata of Jewish high society and lived in the better sections of Jerusalem. . . . They inhabited the country club ionosphere of the city's 'velvet alleys' where they breathed the rarified air of religious piety and unimpeachable integrity. . . . They didn't have an arsenal where they stashed tommy guns and blackjacks and knives and rubber hoses. . . . And there were no handkerchiefs over their faces, no gloves to cover their fingerprints. *They wore instead the robes of righteousness*—the cloak of respectability and public trust, and the mantle of high official office.[1]

That point is an important one to understand. The men who had Jesus put to death were the "spiritual leaders" of Judaism. The great irony—and the scriptural accounts have glimpses of this —is that these men used the law, the very law they claimed so scrupulously to obey, as the weapon to kill Jesus. Even while they swelled with righteous indignation and cried that they were protecting the law from this blasphemous man, they violated that law in a dozen ways.

For example, we know that by Sanhedrin law every trial had to be held in daytime, between the morning and the evening sacrifice. We know that by Sanhedrin law every trial also had to be held in a room of the temple. We know that contradictory testimony between two witnesses brought an automatic acquittal of the accused. We know that a man could not be condemned and executed on the same day. We know that a trial could not be held on the day before a Sabbath lest it not be concluded in one day and have to be carried over. We know that no person could be convicted on the basis of his own testimony. We know—and this is an interesting aspect of Jewish law—that a unanimous verdict of the judges automatically brought about an acquittal for the accused, because they felt he had no advocate in court. All of these aspects of the law were violated in the case of Jesus.[2]

Over and over again the leaders of Judaism trampled the law under foot in order to achieve their objective. And yet, even as they did so, they were adhering to other parts of the law with meticulous exactness. Three references in particular give some insight into the character of the men who conspired to put their Savior to death.

Matthew 27. The arrest had been made, and Jesus had been taken to the palace of Caiaphas. Suddenly Judas realized the magnitude of what he had done, and so, Matthew recorded, Judas took back the betrayal money. "I have betrayed the innocent blood," he said. Their response was "What is that to us?" (Matt. 27:4.) In despair Judas cast the pieces of money at their feet, fled from the room, and committed suicide. (See Matt. 27:5.) The next verse even more fully reveals the hypocrisy of the Jewish religious leaders, these "pious criminals," as Wright called them: "The chief priests took the silver pieces, and said, It is not lawful for to put them into the treasury, because it is the price of blood." (Matt. 27:6.) They had no qualms about bribing a man to betray his master. They had no qualms about an illegal conspiracy to kill the Savior, but when they received money they viewed as spiritually tainted, they were horrified at the thought of putting it into the temple treasury, because it was blood money.

John 18. A second indication of the spiritual hardness and inconsistency of these men is found in the Gospel of John. The Sanhedrin knew that, after they had pronounced the judgment and decreed that Jesus must die, they could not crucify him without the help and permission of the Roman officers. So, John recorded, "then led they Jesus from Caiaphas unto the hall of judgment: and it was early; and they themselves went not into the judgment hall, lest they should be defiled; but that they might eat the passover." (John 18:28.) The rabbis believed that if a Jew associated with a Gentile, especially just before the Passover, he was defiled and had to go through a long and involved ritual cleansing. So again the irony strikes us. Riding roughshod over illegalities in the trial was all right. Manipulating the Roman procurator to do their dirty work was acceptable. Even killing their Messiah was of no concern. But to come in contact with a Gentile and risk defilement before the Passover? Perish the thought!

John 19. John gave us another insight into the character of the men who, in their observance of the law, maintained their obsession with the letter of it but totally lost its spirit. After the crucifixion of Jesus and the two thieves was done, "the Jews therefore, because it was the preparation, that the bodies should not remain upon the cross on the sabbath day, (for that sabbath day was an high day,) besought Pilate that their legs might be broken." (John 19:31.) The Mosaic law said that no dead person could be left on the cross on the Sabbath. (See Deut. 21:23.) Spitting in his face during a totally illegal trial was acceptable. Whipping the mob into the frenzied chant of "Crucify him! Crucify him!" was all right. And once on the cross, looking up into his agonized face and taunting him to come down were nothing. But to leave the body hanging on a holy day—God would surely be displeased by such irreverence. The body must come down!

When we understand that kind of hardness in the Jewish leaders, we can better appreciate what Jacob said: "Wherefore, as I said unto you, it must needs be expedient that Christ . . . should come among the Jews, among those *who are the more wicked part of the world;* and they shall crucify him— . . . and *there is none other nation on earth that would crucify their God.*" (2 Ne. 10:3; italics added.) Had Zeus appeared to the Greeks, had Molech appeared to the Moabites, had Ra or Amun appeared to the Egyptians, the people would have danced in the streets to welcome him and sung hymns of joyous praise. No other people would have crucified their god. And the great irony is that the religious leaders did it, as Jesus had prophesied, thinking they had actually done God a service. (See John 16:2.)

"Knowest Thou the Condescension of God?"

When the angel asked Nephi what he saw in vision, he answered, "A virgin, most beautiful and fair above all other virgins." The angel then asked him an important question: "Knowest thou the condescension of God?" (1 Ne. 11:15–16.) That question has interesting implications concerning God the Father, but it also has implications for God the Son. We know this because a little later the angel said to Nephi, "Look and behold the condescension of God!" (1 Ne. 11:26.) Nephi then saw the ministry and death of the Savior. (See vv. 27–33.)

In Moses 1:32–33 we read: "By the word of my power, have I created them, which is mine Only Begotten Son, who is full of grace and truth. And *worlds without number have I created* . . . and *by the Son I created them.*" (Italics added.) Can you imagine what it must have meant for Jesus to be the creator of innumerable worlds, galaxies, perhaps even universes, and to leave that power and glory and majesty and take upon himself the body of an infant who was totally dependent upon others for nourishment, who could suffer pain, and who could be hungry? "Knowest thou the condescension of God?" We begin to sense why the angel asked that question.

Nephi made a significant point related to the idea of the condescension of the Son of God. In 1 Nephi 19:7 he talked about the people trampling under their feet the very God of Israel, and in verse nine he added, "The world, because of their iniquity, shall judge him to be a thing of naught." Think of the irony of that! That statement is incredible—the world would judge the Creator of all the universe to be something insignificant, a nothing. Nephi continued: "Wherefore they scourge him, and he suffereth it; and they smite him, and he suffereth it. Yea, they spit upon him, and he suffereth it, because of his loving kindness and his long-suffering towards the children of men." (1 Ne. 19:9.)

Think of the time when the men mocked him in the palace of Caiaphas where the trial took place. They put a blindfold on him. They slapped him across the face and said, "Prophesy unto us, thou Christ, Who is he that smote thee?" (Matt. 26:68.) All he had to do was raise one finger, and the entire city of Jerusalem could have been obliterated. When they stepped forward and spat in his face (see Matt. 26:67), all he had to do was to speak a word, and the entire solar system could have been annihilated. This is the Man they were dealing with: the Creator of the universe, a member of the Godhead. When the Roman soldiers jammed the crown of thorns onto his head and lashed his back, he stood patiently, and, as Nephi said, "he suffereth it." Yet he could have spoken but a word and destroyed them all.

Why? Why would he endure such degradation? Why suffer it all when he could so easily have stopped it? "Because of his loving kindness . . . towards the children of men." Surely this gives added meaning to the angel's question, "Knowest thou the condescension of God?"

Stunned Sorrow or Joyous Exultation?

Imagine for a moment the scene in Jerusalem immediately after the death of Jesus. Tear-stained cheeks, eyes red with grief, voices hushed and shocked, a numbing sense of unreality—what a pitiful, tragic three days that must have been for Jesus' followers. The Master, the worker of miracles, he who had raised Lazarus from death just a few days before, now lay in a borrowed tomb. It was too incredible to believe; yet they had seen the torn hands and feet, handled the cold body.

But a vision given to Joseph F. Smith in 1918 tells us that, at exactly that same time, a scene of vastly different tone was occurring elsewhere. (See D&C 138.) Even as one group of disciples was hastily preparing the body for burial, another group of disciples was gathered awaiting his arrival from the mortal world: "There were gathered together in one place an innumerable company. . . . I beheld that they were filled with *joy* and *gladness,* and were rejoicing together. . . . While this vast multitude waited and conversed, *rejoicing* . . . , the Son of God appeared. . . . And the saints *rejoiced* in their redemption. . . . *Their countenances shone,* and the radiance from the presence of the Lord rested upon them, and *they sang praises* unto his holy name." (D&C 138:12, 15, 18, 23–24; italics added.)

The assembly included such righteous people as Adam and Eve, Abel, Noah, Abraham, Isaac, and Jacob—famous Old Testament prophets—and Book of Mormon prophets. (See vv. 38–49.) Prophets from this dispensation, such as Joseph Smith and Brigham Young, were also allowed to attend in their premortal state in preparation for their future roles in the work of the kingdom. (See vv. 53, 56.) Those in Jerusalem who, for those three days, could see only death sorrowed; yet those who were dead who saw life rejoiced.

"And He Saw, and Believed"

Finally we come to the Resurrection itself. In the twentieth chapter of his Gospel, John described how Mary came early and found the empty tomb. When she reported that to Peter and John, they both ran to see for themselves. "He [John] stooping down, and looking in, saw the linen clothes lying; yet went he not in. Then cometh Simon Peter following him, and went into the sepulchre, and seeth the linen clothes lie, and the napkin, that was about his head, not lying with the linen clothes, but *wrapped together in a place by itself.*" (John

20:5–7; italics added.) Why did John take note of that? "Then went in also that other disciple, which came first to the sepulchre [John], and *he saw, and believed.*" (John 20:8, italics added.) What did he see that caused him to believe the Resurrection had taken place?

In the quick preparation for burial, Joseph of Arimathaea and the women with him would have wrapped Jesus with long strips of linen in the manner of the Middle East. Finally they would have wrapped one strip around and around his face to cover it. It was that which John saw, "not lying with the linen clothes, but wrapped together in a place by itself." (V. 7). Who wrapped it and folded it and laid it aside? I believe that Jesus laid aside his own burial clothes; he folded them up and laid them aside.

I have been able to visit Jerusalem often. Every time I go into the Garden Tomb and see that empty tomb, I thrill again and understand, I think, what John meant when he said, "He saw, and believed." And the deepest thrill of all is to know that some day, because of what happened in the tomb that first Easter morning, we will come forth from the grave and lay aside and fold up our own burial clothes and know that we too will live forever and ever.

"Did Not Our Heart Burn?"

Luke told us something about the Resurrection that is not recorded in the other Gospels. After Christ has appeared to Peter and John and to the women at the sepulchre, "two of [the disciples] went that same day to a village called Emmaus, which was from Jerusalem about threescore furlongs. And they talked together of all these things which had happened. And it came to pass, that, while they communed together and reasoned, Jesus himself drew near, and went with them. But their eyes were holden that they should not know him.

And he said unto them, What manner of communications are these?" (Luke 24:13–17.)

They were, I am sure, overflowing with the news of the day—what the women had said, what Peter had said, what John had said. It is not surprising then that "one of them, whose name was Cleopas, answering said unto him, Art thou only a stranger in Jerusalem, and hast not known the things which are come to pass there?" (Luke 24:18.) In other words, Cleopas seemed to say, "How can you be in Jerusalem and not know what has happened?" So they explained to him how Jesus of Nazareth had been delivered up and killed; and then they reported the startling things that had been told to them that very morning.

Jesus replied, "O fools, and slow of heart to believe all that the prophets have spoken: Ought not Christ to have suffered these things, and to enter into his glory?" (Luke 24:25–26.) And then, "beginning at Moses and all the prophets, he expounded unto them in all the scriptures the things concerning himself." (Luke 24:27.) Wouldn't you love to have been able to walk along behind the three of them and hear that conversation? I have often wondered to which scriptures he referred. To what things did he point their minds? From which writings of the prophets did he quote? There is no way to know, of course, but here are some possibilities.

He might have referred to Exodus 12, which describes the great Passover and how Israel was delivered from death and from bondage through the blood of the lamb. Would he have reminded them that this was the Passover season, that the true Lamb had just been offered, and that deliverance from spiritual bondage had been brought to pass?

Perhaps Psalm 22 was another scripture he cited. The opening lines are, "My God, my God, why hast thou forsaken me?" (V. 1.) Had they been at the cross? Had they heard that last agonized cry? (See Matt. 27:46.) A few verses later in that same psalm we read, "All they that see me laugh me to scorn: they shoot out the lip [a Hebrew idiom meaning to mock and ridicule], they shake the head, saying, He trusted on the Lord that he would deliver him: let him deliver him, seeing he delighted in him." (Ps. 22:7–8.) Did the disguised Savior gently remind them how some at the cross had mocked him and challenged him to come down if he were truly the Son of God? (See Matt. 27:39–43.) And then in verse sixteen, we read: "For dogs have compassed me: the assembly of the wicked have inclosed me: they pierced my hands and my feet." And verse eighteen, "They part my garments among them, and cast lots upon my vesture." (See Matt. 27:35.) To anyone who had witnessed the Crucifixion, those prophecies would have been electrifying.

Perhaps he pointed their minds to Psalm 41:9: "Yea, mine own familiar friend, in whom I trusted, which did eat of my bread, hath lifted up his heel against me." Certainly these two men knew by now about Judas's betrayal of the Master.

Or perhaps Psalm 69 may have been another scripture he quoted. Verses twenty and twenty-one read, "Reproach hath broken my heart; and I am full of heaviness: and I looked for some to take pity, but there was none; and for comforters, but I found none. They gave me also gall for my meat; and in my thirst they gave me vinegar to drink." Would these men have seen or heard from other witnesses that a soldier gave Jesus vinegar to drink just before he died? (See John 19:29–30.) Did the disciples realize, as John apparently did, that the Savior died of a broken heart?[3] (See John 19:34–35.) What remorse they must have felt as they thought how no one, not even themselves, had stayed through the ordeal to comfort the Master.

These and other Old Testament prophecies would have clearly showed that all was part of the grand design. We don't know how long he walked with them, and we don't know how long they talked, and we don't know which scriptures he cited, but we do know that when he left them, the two disciples recalled that teaching moment, saying, "Did not our heart burn within us . . . while he opened to us the scriptures?" (Luke 24:32.)

What Can We Ever Do?

Study of these special, sacred scriptures and meditation on all these things can fill us with an overwhelming sense of gratitude for what the Savior did. It can bring us to ask the burning question: "Why would he do this for me?" As the hymn says so beautifully:

> I marvel that he would descend from his throne divine,
> To rescue a soul so rebellious and proud as mine.[4]

If we truly come to sense that he did all these things because of love for us, I hope we will have another question: "What could I ever do to repay him for what he has done for me?" Over the years, I have come across three things that I think have particular power in answering that second question.

The first is a parable by Elder James E. Talmage called "The Parable of the Grateful Cat." He told the story of a naturalist in the nineteenth century who had been called to a grand estate in Great Britain to be honored for his contributions in the world of science. He left his cottage early in the morning to go for a walk, and while he was out walking, he saw two boys by the lake. He also heard the frantic meowing of a cat; and so, curious, he walked over to see what was happening. When he arrived he saw the two boys with a mother cat and some kittens. The boys were taking each kitten, tying it up in a rag with a rock, and tossing it into the lake. As you can imagine, the mother cat was frantic watching her kittens being drowned. A little upset, the naturalist asked the boys what they were doing. They said that the mistress of the great estate had an old mother cat that she loved, but she didn't want any more cats around. Whenever the mother cat had a litter, the woman hired the two boys, who were children of some of the servants, to take the kittens to the lake and drown them.

The naturalist said that he would make sure the boys didn't get in trouble, and he took the remaining three kittens and cared for them. To the scientist's surprise, the mother cat behaved as if she understood exactly what was happening. As he walked back to his cottage with the kittens, she ran alongside him, rubbed his leg, and purred happily. He took the kittens into his cottage, gave them some milk, and put them in a warm box.

The next day, when all the company was gathered together in the great house to honor the scientist, suddenly the door pushed open. In came the mother cat with a large fat mouse in her mouth. She walked to the scientist and laid the mouse at his feet. In the words of Elder Talmage, here is the marvelous parable that he drew from this story:

> What think you of the offering, and the purpose that prompted the act? A live mouse, fleshy and fat! Within the cat's power of possible estimation and judgment it was a superlative gift. To her limited understanding no rational creature could feel otherwise than pleased over the present of a meaty mouse. Every sensible cat would be ravenously joyful with such an offering. Beings unable to appreciate a mouse for a meal were unknown to the cat.
>
> Are not our offerings to the Lord—our tithes and our other freewill gifts—as thoroughly unnecessary to His needs as was the mouse to the scientist? But remember that the grateful and sacrificing nature of the cat was enlarged, and in a measure sanctified, by her offering.
>
> Thanks be to God that He gauges the offerings and sacrifices of His children by the standard of their physical

> ability and honest intent rather than by the gradation of His esteemed station. Verily He is God with us; and He both understands and accepts our motives and righteous desires. Our need to serve God is incalculably greater than His need for our service.[5]

That is one answer to the question, What could I ever do to repay Him? The answer is nothing. Nothing I can do could merit what he did for me. But that is only a partial answer.

The second item is an article from a medical magazine about "belaying" in mountain climbing. The belay system is the way a mountain climber protects himself from falls. Someone climbs up first, gets in a firm, secure position, ties the rope tightly around his waist, and calls down to his partner, "You're on belay," which means, "I have you if you fall." The article reported about Alan Czenkusch, a man who ran a climbing school in Colorado for physicians:

> Belaying has brought Czenkusch his best and worst moment in climbing. Czenkusch once fell from a high precipice, yanking out three mechanical supports and pulling his belayer off a ledge. He was stopped, upside down, ten feet from the ground when his spread-eagled belayer arrested the fall with the strength of his outstretched arms.
>
> "Don saved my life," says Czenkusch. "How do you respond to a guy like that? Give him a used climbing rope for a Christmas present? No, *you remember him. You always remember him.*"[6]

What a profound analogy for us. Like the belayer, the Savior stops our traumatic fall toward spiritual destruction and offers us a safe line back to him. And what can we do to repay him? *Always* remember him. In fact, those very words are the words of the sacramental covenant. (See D&C 20:77, 79; 3 Nephi 18:7, 11.) Think what an effect *always* remembering the Savior and what he has done for us would have in our lives. So the fuller answer to the question, "What can I ever do to repay the Savior?" is both nothing, and everything.

The third item that comes to mind when I ask myself the question about repaying the Savior is a poem by an unknown author:

When Jesus came to Golgotha, they hanged him on a tree.
They drove great nails through hands and feet, they made—a calvary!
They crowned him with a crown of thorns, red were his wounds and deep;
For those were crude and cruel days, and human flesh was cheap.

When Jesus came to our town, they simply passed him by.
They never hurt a hair of him! They merely let him die.
For men had grown more tender; they would not give him pain!
They only passed on down the street, and left him standing in the rain.[7]

Our task is to make a lie of that poem in our own lives. The final answer to the question is, The way I repay the Savior is to accept what he did and make it a reality in my life.

Chapter 5

"Among His Own Kin, and in His Own House"

(Mark 6:4)

Even a quick reading of the Gospels and Acts shows that the New Testament writers did not intend to give a comprehensive picture of the personal life or family of Jesus. Their purpose was to portray Jesus as the Christ and to convey the significance of that fact to the world. This intent partially explains why we have almost no information about the early years of Jesus and why references to his family life are scanty and usually incidental to the main narrative. Still, one naturally wonders about Jesus' family, who they were and what they did.

Brothers and Sisters of Jesus

We do know that Jesus had four brothers and more than one sister. The people of Nazareth objected to the divine calling of Jesus on the grounds that he was someone who had grown up in their midst. "Is not this the carpenter's son?" they asked in astonishment. "Is not his mother called Mary? and his brethren, James, and Joses, and Simon, and

Judas? And his sisters, are they not all with us?" (Matt. 13:55–56.) This last verse and its parallel passage in Mark 6:3 contain the only references to the sisters of Jesus in the New Testament, and nothing is known of their involvement with the Church or their attitude toward the Savior.

The brothers of Jesus—or more correctly, the half-brothers of Jesus—receive more mention, however. John relates an interesting event concerning the brethren of Jesus telling us that they did not fully accept him as the Messiah while he was laboring among them: "Now the Jews' feast of tabernacles was at hand. His brethren therefore said unto him [their brother, Jesus], Depart hence, and go into Judaea, that thy disciples also may see the works that thou doest. For there is no man that doeth any thing in secret, and he himself seeketh to be known openly. If thou do these things, shew thyself to the world. For neither did his brethren believe in him." (John 7:2–5.)

The brothers knew something of Jesus' work and miracles and of his following, but they were doubtful themselves, or at least wished him to be more open about his mission. They did not believe in him, which may refer to the claims he made about being the Messiah and the Son of God. In fact, when the people of Nazareth rejected the Savior, he exclaimed, "A prophet is not without honour, but in his own country, and among his own kin, and in his own house." (Mark 6:4.) But evidently the brothers were converted shortly thereafter, for Luke records that immediately after Christ's ascension into heaven, the church met in "prayer and supplication, with the women, and Mary the mother of Jesus, and with his brethren." (Acts 1:14.) Also, Paul includes James in his list of those who had seen the resurrected Lord. (See 1 Cor. 15:7.)

James

More is known about James than any of the other brothers of Jesus. He is mentioned several times in Acts and in the epistles as playing a prominent role in church leadership. For instance, when Peter is imprisoned in Jerusalem and an angel frees him, Peter tells the first group he meets, "Go shew these things unto James, and to the brethren." (Acts 12:17.) James also takes a leading role in the great Jerusalem Council, which debated the issue of circumcision for Gentiles. (See Acts 15.) James was the one who suggested that a letter be drafted outlining the official Church position on this matter. (See Acts 15:13–21.) Some have erroneously assumed that this James was James, the son of Zebedee, who served in the presidency of the early church with Peter and John. That James, however, was killed by Herod in a wave of persecution against the church. (See Acts 12:1–2.) This occurred about A.D. 44, just before Peter's imprisonment and five or six years before the Jerusalem Council.

In his letter to the Galatian saints, Paul refers to James, the Lord's brother, as an apostle (see Gal. 1:19) and classes him, along with Peter and John, as "pillars" of the church (see Gal. 2:9). Some have conjectured from the latter comment of Paul that James, the brother of the Lord, not only became an apostle, but even filled the vacancy in the leadership of the Twelve caused by the martyrdom of James, the son of Zebedee. The fact that James declared the official policy of the church at the Jerusalem Council and that Paul reported to him after one mission (see Acts 21:17–19) would lend added support to that supposition. Of course, based on what we know, it remains conjecture.

James, the brother of Jesus, was also the one who wrote the epistle of James. Not only does this short letter contain some of the great teachings of gospel doctrine, but in it Joseph Smith found the words (see James 1:5–6) that sent him to the Sacred Grove in the spring of 1820. Note in that epistle that James does not refer to himself as the brother of the Lord but as his servant: "James, a servant of God and of the Lord Jesus Christ." (James 1:1.)

Ancient tradition, preserved for us by Eusebius, a Christian historian who lived about A.D. 300, states that James became bishop of the church at Jerusalem and was called James the Just, respected by Jews and Christians as being the most just man alive. It is said that he prayed so often and so long for the people that his knees became as hard as camel knees.[1]

Josephus, a Jewish historian and general who lived during the lifetime of James, mentioned James's death. Ananus, a chief priest who was a Sadducee (the Sadducees violently opposed the resurrection), "assembled the sanhedrim of the judges, and brought before them the brother of Jesus, who was called Christ, whose name was James, and some others, . . . and when he had formed an accusation against them as breakers of the law, he delivered them to be stoned." Ananus soon lost his position as high priest because of this incident.[2]

Jude and Simon

The writer of the epistle of Jude refers to himself this way: "Jude, the servant of Jesus Christ, and the brother of James." (Jude 1:1.) Most scholars assume that the name James refers to the Lord's brother, identifying the writer as the Judas who is another of the Lord's brothers. Though Jude does not call himself an apostle, the fact that his letter has been recognized and accepted from very early times as authoritative suggests that he too may have been an apostle.

Nothing more is recorded of Simon and Joses in the New Testament. Interestingly, another Simon, or Symeon, is mentioned by Eusebius. This Simon, according to tradition, was the son of Clopas, Joseph's brother, and Mary, whom Matthew called "the other Mary" (28:1) and who was one of the women at the cross and one of the first to see the resurrected Christ (see Matt. 27:55–56; 28:1–10; Mark 15:40). This Simon was thus Jesus' cousin. He succeeded James the Lord's brother as bishop of the church in Jerusalem and was finally crucified in the Roman persecutions under the emperor Trajan.[3] The Bible scholars F. N. Peloubet and William Smith say that many have identified this Symeon with Simon the Lord's brother, though this argument is full of difficulties.[4]

Joseph

We know quite a bit about Joseph, Jesus' stepfather, during the early years of his marriage. Matthew tells us that he was of the lineage of King David, that he was a just and considerate man, that in a dream an angel told him who Jesus would be, that he was obedient, and that he gave Jesus his name, which means *savior.* (See Matt. 1.) We know that he took Mary to Bethlehem, where Jesus was born. (See Luke 2:4–6.) Less than two years later, Joseph took his family into Egypt to escape Herod, after being warned in a dream. In Egypt, a dream again told him when to return, and another dream told him to go to Galilee. (See Matt. 2:13–15, 19–22.) Four dreams from God! Joseph must have been an exceptionally visionary and spiritually sensitive man.

Joseph and Mary also attended the Passover in Jerusalem faithfully every year. (See Luke 2:41.) One incident at the Passover, when Jesus was twelve (see Luke 2:42–49), suggests how well Joseph taught the scriptures to his children. Jewish tradition laid the primary emphasis for the education of children, which emphasized study of the Torah, on the father, though the mother could also teach her children the scriptures.[5] So when Jesus was "in the temple, sitting in the midst of the doctors, both hearing them, and asking them questions," and "all that heard him were astonished at his understanding and answers" (vv. 46–47), his ability positively reflected on Joseph's (and also Mary's) understanding of the scriptures and the teaching Jesus had received. Joseph's knowledge that Jesus was Emmanuel (see Matt. 1:23) had undoubtedly lent urgency to Joseph's teaching.

Though the record is silent concerning the later life of Joseph, most scholars assume that he died sometime during the eighteen years between the family's visit to Jerusalem when Jesus was twelve and the beginning of Christ's formal ministry. If Joseph had been alive, he would likely have been mentioned as being at the marriage celebration in Cana (see John 2:1–11) and almost certainly Jesus would not have given John the charge to care for his mother (see John 19:25–27).

Mary

Aside from the reference to Mary meeting with the Church shortly after the ascension of her Son (see Acts 1:14), we have no record of her after the events of the crucifixion. Ancient traditions, which are not always reliable, tell us that Mary associated with the church in Jerusalem for many years, and finally accompanied John to Ephesus, where she eventually died.

But Mary's contribution to the church and to the work of Jesus Christ may be more lasting than most people realize. As mentioned earlier, she contributed to the training of her son Jesus. Her knowledge of the scriptures was thorough, as indicated by her spontaneous words of rejoicing when she met Elizabeth, words that echo numerous passages in the Old Testament. (See Luke 1:46–55.)

Furthermore, Luke frankly admits that he is writing his gospel from material he had gathered from eyewitnesses of Christ's life. (See Luke 1:1–4.) Many Bible scholars believe that Luke gathered these materials for his gospel while Paul was imprisoned in Caesarea for two years, before Paul was sent to Rome for trial before the emperor. (See Acts 24:26–

27.) Caesarea was only about fifty miles northwest of Jerusalem. If Mary was still in Jerusalem, what better source of information concerning the life of the Master could there be than his mother?

Some unique characteristics of Luke's gospel support the possibility that Mary was one of Luke's sources. First, only in Luke is there a detailed record of the story of the birth of Christ. Matthew records the visits of the angel Gabriel and of the later visit of the wise men, but we turn to Luke to read of the manger and the shepherds, the crowded inn and the swaddling clothes. Only in Luke do we find an account of Gabriel's words to the young Mary (see Luke 1:26–38) and of Mary's visit to Elisabeth (see Luke 1:39–56). Luke's Gospel is the only one that relates the nativity (see Luke 2:1–20), the circumcision of Jesus and the inspired declarations of Anna and Simeon in the temple (see Luke 2:21–38), and the teaching of the young Jesus in the temple at the age of twelve. And interestingly enough, Luke, who exhibits some of the most polished and refined Greek in the New Testament, uses a rough Greek filled with Hebraic style in the chapters that tell us of the infancy and childhood of Jesus. So markedly different is it from the rest of his work that it almost seems as if Luke were translating, a concept that would support the idea that Mary supplied the material.

The information about the family of Jesus that has survived the erasing effects of time is sketchy and incomplete. Yet the evidence we do have suggests strongly that the family of the Savior played active and prominent roles in the early development and history of the church of Jesus Christ.

Chapter 6

"Types of Things to Come"

(Mosiah 13:31)

Many in the world and even some in the Church think that the Old Testament reflects a pregospel culture centered around the Mosaic covenant, which was given in place of the gospel laws. Certainly the Israelites, when they rejected the higher law, were given a lesser law. But note what the Lord said about that: "The lesser priesthood continued, which priesthood holdeth the key of the ministering of angels and the *preparatory gospel; which gospel is the gospel of repentance and of baptism, and the remission of sins, and the law of carnal commandments.*" (D&C 84:26–27; italics added.)

They did not receive the *fulness* of the gospel, but they did receive a *preparatory* gospel, dealing with the basic principles of the gospel of Jesus Christ. As Paul taught the Galatian Saints, this was done so that they could be brought to Christ: "Wherefore the law was our schoolmaster to bring us unto Christ, that we might be justified by faith. But after that faith is come, we are no longer under a schoolmaster." (Gal. 3:24–25.)

In short, the Old Testament is not pregospel but primary gospel; and we can expect that the Old Testament, especially in its types and symbols, will richly reflect that gospel, the gospel of preparation for faith in Christ. It can be a preparation of value to every person, including those who have access to, though possibly not complete understanding of, the fulness of the gospel. Therefore, as Elder Bruce R. McConkie suggests, "It is wholesome and proper to look for similitudes of Christ everywhere and to use them repeatedly in keeping him and his laws uppermost in our minds."[1]

The question comes to mind, then, When is an act or object recorded in scripture to be taken literally and when should it be interpreted figuratively? Symbols can be taken too literally, and their true meaning lost in a grotesque parody of reality. On the other hand, sometimes one can explain away the actual meaning of a passage by saying it is only figurative. The following guidelines may be helpful as one tries to decide how to interpret correctly the symbols used in the Old Testament:

1. Look for the interpretation of the symbol in the scriptures themselves.

2. Look for Christ in the symbols and imagery of the scriptures.

3. Let the nature of the object used as a symbol contribute to your understanding of its spiritual meaning.

4. Seek the reality behind the symbol. One author used this interesting analogy about reality and representing reality through symbols:

> The most perfect representation of a steam-engine to a South-sea savage would be wholly and hopelessly unintelligible to him, simply because the reality, the outline of which was presented to him, was something hitherto unknown. But let the same drawing be shewn to those who have seen the reality, such will have no difficulty in explaining the representation. And the greater the acquaintance with the reality, the greater will be the ability to

> explain the picture. The savage who had never seen the steam-engine would of course know nothing whatever about it. Those who had seen an engine but know nothing of its principles, though they might tell the general object of the drawing, could not explain the details. But the engineer, to whom every screw and bolt are familiar, to whom the use and the object of each part is thoroughly known, would not only point out where each of these was to be found in the picture, but would shew what others might overlook, how in different engines these might be made to differ.[2]

The reality behind the Old Testament is Jesus Christ and his teachings of salvation. The better we understand him, the more clearly we will see the meaning of the symbols.

The preliminary exploration of Old Testament types and symbols that follows deals with different kinds of ordinances, festivals, and historical events. Of course, space does not permit more than a sampling of the full range of symbols available in the Mosaic covenant.

Ordinances

Sacrifices and Offerings. Sacrifices and offerings represent the very center of the Mosaic law. Though they varied in the manner of offering, the requirements, the item offered, and the time of offering, all of the sacrifices and offerings had three general things in common: an offerer, the offering, and the priesthood. Adam was taught that the law of sacrifice was instituted as "a similitude of the sacrifice of the Only Begotten of the Father." (Moses 5:7.) The similitude of Christ's sacrifice carries through all three aspects. One author explained the typology of all three aspects in this manner:

> What, then, is *the offering?* what *the priest?* what *the offerer?* Christ is the offering, Christ is the priest, Christ is the offerer. Such and so manifold are the relations in which Christ has stood for man and to man, that no one type or

> set of types can adequately represent the fulness of them. . . . As man under the law, our substitute, Christ stood for us towards God as offerer. . . . Thus His body was His offering: he willingly offered it; and then as priest He took the blood into the holiest. As *offerer,* we see Him *man under the law,* standing our substitute, for us to fulfil all righteousness. As *priest,* we have Him presented as the *mediator,* God's messenger between Himself and Israel. While as *the offering* He is seen *the innocent victim,* a sweet savour to God, yet bearing the sin and dying for it.[3]

Nephi taught that we are to follow the example of the Son of God. (See 2 Ne. 31:10, 12–13, 16.) Jesus asked, "What manner of men ought ye to be?" and then answered his own question by saying, "Even as I am." (3 Ne. 27:27.) If Christ becomes our model for living, then in the three aspects of the law of the offerings, we too should be typified. In other words, just as all three objects and persons involved in the sacrifices were types of him, they should also serve as types of us.

Thus, the offering becomes a type or symbol of our lives, our acts, our works, our very being – our all – offered to God on the altar so that it becomes a sweet-smelling savor to him. The Saints are to become "kings and priests" (Rev. 1:6), or as Peter said, "a royal priesthood" (1 Pet. 2:9). Further, like Jesus they are to become the saviors of men by sharing with others the principles of his teachings and sacrifice. (See D&C 103:9–10.) In this manner they are typified by the priest. The offerer also typifies us as well as Christ, for, like him, we must willingly yield ourselves to come into the proper relationship with God.[4]

Circumcision. Abraham was specifically commanded by the Lord to institute circumcision upon himself and all the males of his household as a token of the covenant made with God. (See Gen. 17:9–14.) In the Joseph Smith Translation of the Bible of this passage, we learn that circumcision was instituted as a token of the covenant; but the token was given because the people were in a state of apostasy, had lost sight of the true meaning of the ordinance of baptism, and were washing their children and sprinkling them with blood so that they would be free from sin. Circumcision reminded the people that, while children were born in the covenant, they were not to be held accountable until they reached eight years of age. (See JST Gen. 17:4–11.)

Other scriptures provide additional clarification that it was not circumcision itself but what it stood for that gave it its greatest significance. In many places the Lord speaks of true circumcision as being circumcision of the heart or, in other words, loving God and being obedient to the Spirit. The "uncircumcised of heart" are the wicked, proud, and rebellious. (See Deut. 10:16; 30:6; Jer. 4:4; Ezek. 44:7; Acts 7:51; Rom. 2:25–29; Col. 2:11.) Though a person may be circumcised in the flesh, unless he is righteous the covenant is invalidated, and the circumcision becomes profitless. Thus, circumcision was only a sign or token of what needed to happen to the inward man. If the inward change had not taken place, then circumcision was virtually meaningless. Following the atonement of Christ, the token of circumcision was no longer required of God's covenant people since baptism, the symbol of Christ's own death and resurrection, replaced it. (See Jer. 9:25–26; Acts 15:22–29; 1 Cor. 7:19; Gal. 5:1–6; 6:12–15; Philip. 3:3–4.)

The Abrahamic covenant makes frequent reference to one's seed. (See, for example, Genesis 17:6–12.) The organ of the male body that produces seed and helps bring about physical birth is the very part of the body that bears the token of the covenant. However, the organ of spiritual rebirth is the heart. (See 3 Ne. 9:20.) Thus, when a person was circumcised it signified that he, like a child, was born into the covenant but need not be baptized until he became accountable before the Lord. But spiritual circumcision, or the circumcision of the heart, must take place once one becomes accountable; otherwise, one is not considered as truly belonging to Israel. As Paul said so aptly, "For he is not a Jew, which is one outwardly; neither is that circumcision, which is outward in the flesh: but he is a Jew, which is one inwardly; and circumcision is that of the heart, in the spirit, and not in the letter; whose praise is not of men, but of God." (Rom. 2:28–29.)

Cleansing of the Leper. In Leviticus 14 we have a detailed description of the ritual that was to take place when a person's leprosy had been healed. Because of the nature of the ritual, many people have seen it as a primitive, superstitious, and abhorrent rite, which demonstrates that the Israelites were scarcely more than barbaric. However, when we apply our guidelines for interpreting symbols, we find that the ritual is a beautiful representation of gospel truths. This case is worth examining in some detail in its twelve major features:

1. *The leper.* Leprosy in its various forms was a loathsome disease causing decay and putrefaction of the living body. It required the sufferer to be ostracized and cut off from any fellowship with the rest of the house of Israel. Because of these characteristics, leprosy was also an appropriate type or symbol of what happens to a man spiritually when he sins. Sin introduces decay and corruption into the spiritual realm, just as leprosy does into the physical. Also, a sinful person was cut off from fellowship with spiritual Israel and could not be part of the Lord's covenant people. So the leper himself provided a type or similitude of what King Benjamin called the "natural man." (See Mosiah 3:19.)

2. *The priest.* The priest served as the official representative of the Lord, authorized to pronounce the leper clean and bring him back into full fellowship. As we have seen earlier, the priest was also a type of Christ.

3. *The birds.* The birds used in the ritual of cleansing symbolized the candidate. Because two truths were to be taught, two birds were required. The first bird was killed by the shedding of its blood, signifying that the leper (the natural man) had to give up his life. The second bird, after being bound together with other symbols, was released, signifying that the man had been freed from the bondage of sin.

4. *The cedar wood.* The cedar wood, along with the living bird, a piece of wool, and a branch of hyssop, were dipped in the blood of the sacrificed bird. Cedar wood is still used today because of its ability to resist decay and corruption. It signified that, once the man had been freed from sin through sacrifice, he ought to preserve himself from spiritual corruption.

5. *The scarlet wool.* The word *scarlet* in Leviticus 14:4 really means a piece of wool dyed bright red, a reminder of blood, which is the symbol of life and also of atonement. (See Lev. 17:11.)

6. *The hyssop.* Though we are not sure exactly why, we do know that in Old Testament times the woody herb hyssop was used in purification rituals to sprinkle blood or water. (See Ex. 12:22; Ps. 51:7; Heb. 9:19.) It was one of most insignificant and unimposing shrubs in Palestine and was often associated with humility.[5] Thus the use of the hyssop stressed the necessity of humility in sacrifice, as well as purification.

7. *The basin of water.* Notice that the blood of the bird was mixed with water. In Moses 6:59 we learn that blood and water are the symbols of birth, both physical and spiritual. Also, we know that the baptismal font, the place of spiritual rebirth, symbolizes the place where the natural man is put to death and the new spiritual man is born. (See Rom. 6:1–6; D&C 128:12–13.) The first bird was killed over the basin of water, symbolizing the death of the natural man and the eventual rebirth of the spiritually innocent person.

8. *The washing of the leper.* Both physically and spiritually, the washing was a symbol of cleansing. This symbol of cleansing through washing is one of the most common in priesthood ordinances, found in baptism, washing and anointing, and washing of feet, for example.

9. *The shaving of the hair.* This act, including even the eyebrows, would make a person look very much like a newborn infant, who typically is virtually without hair. Thus, after going through the process of rebirth symbolically, the candidate graphically demonstrated on his own person that he was newborn spiritually.

10. *The sacrifice of the lamb.* The typology of the sacrifice of the lamb is clear, since the lamb offered had to be the firstborn male without spot or blemish. It symbolized the offering of the Son of God himself.

11. *The smearing of the blood on the parts of the body.* In Hebrew the word which is usually translated *atonement* literally means "to cover." Thus, when the priest touched something with the blood, his action suggested the sanctification of, or atonement made for, that thing. In this case we find the blood of the lamb sanctifying the ear, the organ of hearing representing obedience; the hand, the organ of action; and the foot, the organ of motion representing walking in the proper way. Thus, every aspect of the person's life was touched and affected by the atonement of Christ.

12. *The oil.* "The olive tree from the earliest times has been the emblem of peace and purity."[6] Also, in the Parable of the Ten Virgins, the wise were prepared with oil. (See Matt. 25:1–13.) Modern revelation equates that preparation (having olive oil) with taking "the Holy Spirit for their guide." (D&C 45:55–57.) To touch with oil suggests the effect of the Spirit on the same organs of living and acting that had previously been cleansed by the blood of Christ. Thus, every aspect of the candidate's life was purified and sanctified by both the Atonement and the Holy Ghost.

Feasts and Festivals

Special holidays and festivals were a common part of everyday life during biblical times, and many of them were mandated by the Mosaic law. Thus, unlike modern times, most of the feasts and festivals had religious significance and were an inseparable part of worship.

The Sabbath. Certainly the most frequent festival among the Hebrews was the weekly day of rest, instituted in similitude of what God had done during the creation of the earth when, we are told, the Lord sanctified the Sabbath and rested. (See Gen. 2:2–3.)

In Exodus 31:13 the Lord revealed the basic key to understanding the significance of the Sabbath: "Verily my sabbaths ye shall keep: *for it is a sign* between me and you throughout your generations; *that ye may know that I am the Lord that doth sanctify you.*" (Italics added.) In other words, the Sabbath is the day that man ceases his labors so that God can work his own work – the work of sanctification – on man. The requirement of a sabbatical year, that the land be left untilled, required man to exercise tremendous faith in God's ability to sustain his people both temporally and spiritually. (See Lev. 25:1–7, 18–22.) The promises of abundance and closeness to the Lord for those who keep the Sabbath are beautifully outlined by Isaiah and in modern revelation. (See Isa. 58:13–14; D&C 59:9–24.)

The Feast of the Passover. Passover (which included the Feast of Unleavened Bread) was one of the festivals that most clearly offered typologies of Christ and his atoning sacrifice. It commemorated the night when Jehovah delivered Israel from bondage in Egypt. The actual events of that night of deliverance are recalled during the Feast of the Passover by the meal and the ritual the family performs before the meal.

In spite of the great power demonstrated by Moses, again

and again Pharaoh had hardened his heart and refused to let Israel go. Finally, in the spring, the time when all nature seems to be coming to life again, the Lord revealed to Moses the final steps they must take to be delivered from bondage. This remarkable event involved numerous items, all of which have typological significance, especially when one remembers that Israel's state of slavery was itself a type of our bondage to sin and Satan.

1. *A new beginning.* The Lord indicated that Israel's calendar was to begin its cycle from this event, which was to be the beginning of the year. (See Ex. 12:2.) Symbolically speaking, the deliverance from the bondage of sin marks a new beginning, a new time, a new life, as it were.

2. *The lamb.* On the tenth day of the month, a lamb was chosen and, in the evening of the fourteenth day, was sacrificed. (See Ex. 12:3–6.) The lamb's typology of Jesus Christ's sacrifice is obvious. The animal had to be a male without any defects or blemishes. Each household in Israel was to take such a lamb, signifying that the coming deliverance from the angel of death applied to every household of the covenant.

3. *Blood applied by the hyssop.* Moses specified that each householder must place the blood on the door frame using the herb hyssop, a symbol of purification, as a brush or dauber. (See Ex. 12:22.) These instructions suggest two things: since the doorway to the home is the entry to be guarded if enemies are to be kept out, not only did the blood of the lamb keep out the angel of death (see Ex. 12:13), but the blood on the lintels and sideposts also overshadowed every entrance and exit of an individual—every thought, word, and action. Is this not related to the modern commandment that all of our ingoings and outgoings should be in the name of the Lord? (See D&C 109:17–18.)

4. *The meal.* The family would then roast the entire lamb and consume it with unleavened bread and bitter herbs. Any-

thing left of the lamb (the inedible parts, such as bones, feet, and so on) were to be burned with fire. (See Ex. 12:10; see also Elder McConkie's statement later on the significance of fire.) As the Lamb of God gave himself wholly to be sacrificed for the sins of the world, so must the *paschal* lamb (from *pesach,* the Hebrew word for passover) be wholly consumed. When food is eaten, it goes into the body and literally becomes part of us, sustaining life and giving us strength. So with the atoning sacrifice of the Savior: it must be partaken of and absorbed entirely so as to provide spiritual life and strength.

The Jews saw the bitter herbs as a reminder of the bitterness of their bondage in Egypt. The unleavened bread has its own significance. Leaven, or yeast, is a symbol of corruption because of its tendency to spoil. Christ warned the disciples about the leaven of the Pharisees and the Sadducees, defining it as their false teachings and their hypocrisy. (See Matt. 16:6–12; Mark 8:15; Luke 12:1.) Following the actual Passover, the Israelites were commanded to observe the Feast of the Unleavened Bread, not only abstaining from any leaven for seven days, but also purging it out of their houses. (See Ex. 12:18–19.) Knowing that leaven is a type or symbol of corruption helps us see the beauty of this requirement. After deliverance from death and bondage by the blood of the Lamb, we are to purge all wickedness, pride, and hypocrisy from our lives. Paul also drew on the typology of leaven to teach about Christ. (See 1 Cor. 5:7–8.)

5. *Eating with haste.* The feast was to be eaten hastily, with loins girded, shoes on the feet (which was contrary to normal custom), and staff in hand. (See Ex. 12:11.) The typology here is quite obvious: when the Lord delivers us from the bondage of sin, there must be no tarrying, no delay.

At midnight the angel of death smote all the first born of the land but "passed over" the houses of the children of

Israel marked by the blood of the lamb. (See Ex. 12:29.) Our deliverance from the angel of spiritual death comes only when we have partaken of the "flesh and blood" of the Lamb of God and have metaphorically placed his blood on the doorposts of our lives so that it overshadows all we do. We note also that Pharaoh (a type of Satan) absolutely refused to let Israel go free. The only thing that changed his mind was the death of the firstborn son. (See Ex. 12:30–32.)

The Feast of Weeks. On the fiftieth day after Passover (a period of seven weeks of seven days, or a sabbath of weeks) a second major festival was held, though it lasted only one day. Christians are more familiar with this feast by its Greek title, Pentecost, which means "fiftieth." Elder McConkie explains in detail its important typology:

> The Lord chose the Pentecost, which grew out of the final Passover, as the occasion to dramatize forever the fulfillment of all that was involved in the sacrificial fires of the past. Fire is a cleansing agent. Filth and disease die in its flames. The baptism of fire, which John promised Christ would bring, means that when men receive the actual companionship of the Holy Spirit, then evil and iniquity are burned out of their souls as though by fire. The sanctifying power of that member of the Godhead makes them clean. In similar imagery, all the fires on all the altars of the past, as they burned the flesh of animals, were signifying that spiritual purification would come by the Holy Ghost, whom the Father would send because of the Son. On the first Pentecost of the so-called Christian Era such fires would have performed their purifying symbolism if the old order had still prevailed. How fitting it was instead for the Lord to choose that very day to send living fire from heaven, as it were, fire that would dwell in the hearts of men and replace forever all the fires on all the altars of the past. And so it was that "when the day of Pentecost was fully come, they were all with one accord in one place. And suddenly there came a sound from heaven as of a rushing mighty

wind, and it filled all the house where they were sitting. And there appeared unto them cloven tongues like as of fire, and it sat upon each of them. And they were all filled with the Holy Ghost." (Acts 2:1–4.)[7]

The Day of Atonement. The most sacred and solemn of all Israelite festivals was the Day of Atonement, which took place each autumn. In it, the typology or symbolism of Christ's work for Israel fairly shines. A day of national fasting, it signified that the sins of Israel had been atoned for and that the nation and its people were restored to fellowship with God. The feast included the following major items as detailed in Leviticus 16:

1. *The high priest.* The high priest had to go through meticulous preparation to be worthy to act as officiator for the rest of the house of Israel. He made sacrifices for himself and his house, as well as washing various objects in the tabernacle and purifying them through the sprinkling of sacrificial blood.

The high priest put off the official robes he normally wore and clothed himself in simple, white linen garments, signifying "the righteousness of saints." (Rev. 19:8.) The apostle Paul in the book of Hebrews drew heavily on the typology of the Day of Atonement to teach the mission of Christ. In that epistle he pointed out that Christ is the great "High Priest" who, unlike the high priest of the Aaronic Priesthood, was holy and without spot and did not need to make atonement for his own sins before he could be worthy to officiate for Israel and enter the Holy of Holies. (See Heb. 3:1; 7:26–27.) His perfect life was the ultimate fulfillment of the symbol of wearing white garments.

2. *The goats.* Two goats were chosen by lot. One was designated as the goat of the Lord, and one was designated as the scapegoat or, in Hebrew, the goat of *Azazel.* The goat of Jehovah was offered as a sin offering, and the high priest

took its blood into the Holy of Holies of the tabernacle and sprinkled it on the lid of the ark of the covenant (called the "mercy seat"), thus making atonement for the sins of Israel.

The other goat, *Azazel,* was brought before the high priest, who laid his hands upon its head and symbolically transferred all of the sins of Israel to it. Then it was taken out into the wilderness and released where it would never be seen again. Commentators explain the significance of *Azazel* by saying that it represented "the devil himself, the head of the fallen angels, who was afterwards called Satan; for no subordinate evil spirit could have been placed in antithesis to Jehovah . . . , but only the ruler or head of the kingdom of demons."[8]

3. *The temple.* The rituals of the Day of Atonement took place in the tabernacle and later the temple and culminated when the high priest entered the most sacred room, the Holy of Holies, which was entered but once a year, on this day. The true tabernacle (or temple, or house of the Lord) in which the priest officiated is in heaven, and the earthly tabernacle made by Moses was a "shadow" or type of the "heavenly" one. (See Heb. 8:2–5; 9:1–9.)

Christ, as the lamb of Jehovah as well as High Priest, shed his own blood to enter the heavenly Holy of Holies where that blood ransomed from their sins those who would believe in him and obey his commandments. (See Heb. 9:11–14, 24–28; 10:11–22; D&C 45:3–5.)

The Feast of Tabernacles. The third of the national feasts requiring the attendance of all males was the Feast of Tabernacles (Hebrew *Sukkoth*), which took place five days after the Day of Atonement. It was a celebration of the completion of the harvest and was a time of great joy and thanksgiving. During the week of the festival, Israel was required to live in homemade tabernacles rather than in their homes, a reminder that they had dwelt in tents or tabernacles (King

James translation uses the word *booth*) when the Lord brought them out of Egypt. (See Lev. 23:42–43.)

Elder McConkie points out that this will be the only Mosaic feast reinstituted in this gospel dispensation:

> In the full sense, it is the Feast of Jehovah, the one Mosaic celebration which, as part of the restitution of all things, shall be restored when Jehovah comes to reign personally upon the earth for a thousand years. Even now we perform one of its chief rituals in our solemn assemblies, the giving of the Hosanna Shout, and the worshipers of Jehovah shall yet be privileged to exult in other of its sacred rituals. . . . The fact that it celebrated the completion of the full harvest symbolizes the gospel reality that it is the mission of the house of Israel to gather all nations to Jehovah, a process that is now going forward, but will not be completed until that millennial day when "the Lord shall be king over all the earth," and shall reign personally thereon.[9]

Actual Historical Events

Nephi taught that "all things which have been given of God from the beginning of the world, unto man, are the typifying of [Christ]." (2 Ne. 11:4.) One cannot read far into the Old Testament without discovering that Nephi's phrase "all things" even includes actual historical events. We know that God raises up men for special purposes and uses nations to bring about his will. He calls Assyria "the rod of mine anger" (Isa. 10:5–7), Cyrus of Persia the "anointed" of the Lord (Isa. 45:1), and Nebuchadnezzar's kingdom a gift from "the God of heaven" (Dan. 2:37). But many people do not look beyond that kind of direct intervention in historical events to see that the Lord may also influence events in such a way that they take on symbolic significance. This does not, of course, suggest that the events did not happen as described. Rather, it means that in the reality of the events we also find the Lord's hand at work, giving history symbolical as well as historical significance.

The Testing of Abraham. Most people immediately see in Abraham's test the symbolism of the divine Father offering his only Son, but many miss the precision of detail that God used to show what he himself would have to do in the future with his own Son. Abraham, for instance, was obviously a type or similitude of the Father. Interestingly enough, his name *Abram* means "exalted father," and *Abraham* means "father of a great multitude." (Gen. 17:5.)

Isaac was a type of the Son of God. (See Jacob 4:5.) Note that, like Jesus, he was the product of a miraculous birth. Though not the literal son of God, like Jesus, Isaac was conceived through the intervention of God. Paul called Isaac "his [Abraham's] only begotten son" when he referred to this event. (Heb. 11:17.)

Not only did the Lord ask Abraham to perform the act that would mirror the Redeemer's own future actions, but he also designated a specific place, Moriah—"upon one of the mountains which I will tell thee of." (Gen. 22:2.) Mount Moriah today is one of the three major hills or mounts of Jerusalem. The traditional site where Abraham offered Isaac is one occupied today by the Dome of the Rock, a beautiful Arab mosque. A few hundred yards to the north on that same ridge is another world-famous site known as Gordon's Calvary. Its Hebrew name was Golgotha. The specific location further strengthens the symbolism and emphasizes the similarities between the two sacrifices. In other words, not only did Abraham offer Isaac in similitude of the Father's sacrifice of his own Son, but also he did it in the very place where the later sacrifice would occur.

When they arrived at Moriah, the Genesis account says that Abraham "took the wood of the burnt offering, and laid it upon Isaac his son." (Gen. 22:6.) The Joseph Smith Translation is even more specific: "laid it upon his back." (JST Gen. 22:7.) Some have seen here a similarity to Christ's carrying of the cross upon his shoulders on the way to the crucifixion.[10] Note also that both Christ and Isaac were "bound." (Gen. 22:9; Matt. 27:2.)

One important aspect often overlooked is Isaac's voluntary submission to Abraham. The Old Testament does not give us enough detail to determine exactly how old Isaac was at the time of this event, but it is very likely that he was an adult, since, immediately following the account of the sacrifice on Mount Moriah, we are told that Sarah died at the age of 127. (See Gen. 23:1.) That would have made Isaac thirty-seven at the time of her death. Even if this journey to Moriah had happened several years before her death, Isaac would have been in his thirties. But the exact age is not really important. What is significant is that Abraham was well over a hundred years old, and Isaac, almost certainly no child, could have put up a fierce resistance had he chosen to do so. Instead, he submitted willingly to his father, as the Savior willingly did to his Father.

Once the intended sacrifice had been accepted, Abraham named the place *Jehovah-jireh,* which the King James Version translates as "in the mount of the Lord it shall be seen." (Gen. 22:14.) Adam Clarke, citing other scholars, says the proper translation should be "on this mount the Lord shall be seen." Clarke then concludes:

> From this it appears, that the sacrifice offered by Abraham was understood to be a *representative* one, and a tradition was kept up, that Jehovah should be seen in a sacrificial way on this mount. And this renders . . . more than probably . . . that Abraham offered Isaac on that *very mountain,* on which, in the fulness of time, Jesus suffered.[11]

Two other scholars, C. F. Keil and F. Delitzsch, not only note the significance of the site for the sacrifice of Jesus himself, but also point out that it relates to the site of Solomon's temple: "The place of sacrifice points with peculiar clearness [to] Mount Moriah, upon which under the legal economy *all the typical sacrifices were offered to Jehovah; . . . that by this one true sacrifice the shadows of the typical sacrifices might be rendered both real and true.*"[12]

The Exodus. In addition to the Passover, the events of Israel's deliverance from Egypt and its eventual return to the promised land contain many great and significant types and similitudes. The Lord can influence history so that the events themselves take on the nature of a similitude and provide us with important symbols and types. Note the following events which became part of the Exodus experience:

1. *Bondage to Egypt.* The very situation itself that led to the Exodus is a type of the children of God. Israel, the Lord's chosen people, was in bondage to an evil power. Note how Egypt, like Babylon, is used as a symbol of the world or spiritual wickedness. (See Rev. 11:8.) Also note how frequently sin is compared to bondage and how consistently Satan's power is acknowledged. (See, for example, Rom. 6:12; 7:15; 2 Ne. 1:18; 2:29; 28:22–23; Alma 12:11; 34:35.)

2. *The parting of the Red Sea.* At the command of the Lord, Moses stretched out his hand and the Red Sea parted, making a way for the Israelites to pass through the water and escape destruction. (See Ex. 14:15–31.) The only way a person can escape spiritual death and the bondage of sin is to demonstrate faith in Christ to the point of true repentance so that he can be "buried" in the waters of baptism and be born again by being drawn forth from those waters. (See Rom. 6:1–6; John 3:3–5; Mosiah 27:24–25.)

3. *A pillar of fire and smoke.* In the Exodus, the angel of God went before the Israelites in the form of a pillar of fire and smoke that overshadowed them by night and day. (See Ex. 13:20–22; 14:19.) Being baptized of water is not sufficient

to save a person; he must also receive the Holy Ghost, whose influence and presence are symbolized, among other things, by fire and burning. (See, for example, Acts 2:3–4; D&C 9:8–9.) Receiving the Holy Ghost after baptism is likened to being baptized by fire. (See Matt. 3:11; 2 Ne. 31:17.) As part of their deliverance from the slavery of Egypt, the Israelites were saved both by passing through water and by being overshadowed by fire.

4. *Manna.* In the wilderness, the Israelites were sustained by the manna God sent forth, specifically called "bread from heaven." (Ex. 16:4.) In the great "Bread of Life" sermon, Jesus pointedly taught that he was "the living bread which came down from heaven" (John 6:51); and John the Revelator promised certain faithful Saints that they could eat of "hidden manna" (Rev. 2:17).

5. *Rebellion or obedience.* In the wilderness, God provided Israel with his law and instructed Moses to build a tabernacle, or portable temple, so that the Lord could dwell in their midst. (See Ex. 19–31.) But rebellious Israel demanded that Aaron make them false gods to worship. (See Ex. 32.) For this and repeated rebellions, many Israelites were destroyed, a law of carnal commandments was given, and they were denied the full power of the priesthood. (See D&C 84:24–27.) Later, for further lack of faith, all adults but two were denied access to the promised land and made to wander in the wilderness for forty years. (See Num. 14:30.) Clearly, these events teach us that deliverance from the bondage of sin through baptism and receiving the Holy Ghost is not enough. We must maintain faith in the Lord and hearken to his commandments or lose the promised blessings. As Nephi taught, baptism is only the gate to the straight and narrow path, and we must "press forward with a steadfastness in Christ" if we are to achieve eternal life. (2 Ne. 31:17–20.)

6. *Water from the rock.* In the wilderness of Zin, the Isra-

elites ran out of water to drink and once again began to murmur to Moses. By command of the Lord, Moses and Aaron gathered the people before a rock, Moses smote it, water came forth, and Israel lived. (See Ex. 17:1–7.) At the well in Samaria, Jesus told the woman of the "living water" he could give, which, if partaken of, would become "a well of water springing up into everlasting life." (John 4:14.) In the closing parable of the Sermon on the Mount, Jesus likened his teachings to a rock. Moses and other Old Testament prophets called Jehovah the Rock of salvation. (See, for example, Deut. 32:4, 15, 18; 2 Sam. 22:3, 47; Ps. 18:2, 31, 46.) Thus we see that, when Israel hungered, they were fed the bread that came down from heaven and when they thirsted they received the waters of life from the Rock.

7. *Fiery serpents.* While wandering in the wilderness, the Israelites were also afflicted with a plague of fiery serpents, and many died. The Lord told Moses to make a brass serpent and place it on a pole so that, if a person were bitten, he could look upon the brass serpent and would live. (See Num. 21:6–9.) How can one miss the typology of that event? The covenant people, wandering in the wilderness (notice the similarity to Lehi's dream, 1 Ne. 8:4) because of rebellion, were being bitten by serpents (a symbol for Satan) and were suffering death. To be saved, they looked to a figure lifted up on a pole, and death was averted. Again, the evidence is clear that this event had more than mere historical coincidence. (See John 3:14–15; 2 Ne. 25:25; Alma 33:19–21; Hel. 8:14–15.)

Paul synthesized the events of the Exodus when he said, "Moreover, brethren, I would not that ye should be ignorant, how that all our fathers were under the cloud, and all passed through the sea; and *were all baptized* unto Moses *in the cloud and in the sea;* and did all eat the same spiritual meat; and did all drink the same spiritual drink: for they drank of that spiritual Rock that followed them: *and that Rock was Christ."* (1 Cor. 10:1–4; italics added.)

Entry into the Promised Land. The period when the children of Israel crossed over Jordan and entered the promised land is also full of typology. Obviously, the ultimate promise is the celestial kingdom, but one also enters a new land (or life) when he is born again through baptism. (See Alma 37:45.) With that in mind, notice the following interesting items associated with that event:

1. *Joshua.* The person who led Israel into the promised land was Joshua, whose Hebrew name is *Yehoshua* or *Yeshua.* When Greek became the dominant language of the Middle East, the name *Yehoshua* was transliterated into *Hee-ay-sous,* which in English became *Jesus.* But Jesus' Hebrew name was *Yehoshua* or *Joshua,* which interestingly enough means "God is help" or "Jehovah saves." Notice that twice in the New Testament the name Jesus is used when the speaker obviously means Joshua. (See Acts 7:45; Heb. 4:8.) So "Jesus" led Israel into the promised land.

2. *Put to death.* Anyone who rebelled against the leadership of Joshua and refused to cross over Jordan was to "be put to death." (Josh. 1:18.) Anyone who refuses to follow Jesus into the celestial kingdom will suffer some degree of spiritual death. That is, he will be separated from the presence of God.

3. *Sanctifying oneself.* Joshua called upon the people to sanctify themselves so they would be worthy to go into the promised land. (See Josh. 3:5.) One must be sanctified, or cleansed from sin, in order to enter a new life with God.

4. *The ark of the covenant entering the promised land.* The ark of the covenant, which symbolized the presence of Jehovah, went before the camp of Israel and led the way into the new land. (See Josh. 3:11.) Like passing through the Red Sea, Israel again passed through the midst of the waters to enter

the promised land. (See Josh. 3:15–17.) The Lord specifically connected the two events by asking that a memorial be built. (See Josh. 4:20–24.) The crossing of Israel into the new land was also done on the first day of passover (see Josh. 4:19; Ex. 12:2–3), again invoking the typology of deliverance from bondage and death.

5. *Circumcision reinstituted.* Once they entered into the promised land, Joshua was commanded to perform the ordinance of circumcision among the Israelites. (See Josh. 5:2–7.) While wandering in the wilderness, this token of the Abrahamic covenant had not been performed. Now that they had sanctified themselves and followed Jesus (seen in the types of Joshua and the ark of the covenant) into the promised land, they were once again the true covenant people, so therefore the token was reinstituted.

Thus we see that both the Exodus, including the Passover, and the entry into Canaan have great typological significance. In actuality the whole exodus from slavery to entry into the promised land provides a type or similitude of what must happen to each individual if he is to "[put] off the natural man and [become] a saint through the atonement of Christ the Lord." (Mosiah 3:19.)

One does not go to a great museum like the Smithsonian in Washington, D.C., and fully explore its treasures in an hour or two. Similarly, one does not exhaust the typology of the Old Testament in so brief a presentation as this. Seeing how the Old Testament points to and anticipates Jesus Christ requires a lifetime of exploration and pondering. The Lord revealed to what extent he has filled the treasure house when he said, "*All things have their likeness, and all things are created and made to bear record of me, both things which are temporal, and things which are spiritual; things which are in the heavens above, and things which are on the earth, and things which are in the earth, and things which are under the earth, both above and beneath: all things bear record of me.*" (Moses 6:63; italics added.)

Chapter 7

"His Name Shall Be Called . . ."

(Isaiah 9:6)

After Israel had been captive in Egypt for four hundred years, Jehovah called to Moses out of the burning bush and commanded him to deliver the children of Israel. Moses asked an intriguing question of the Lord: "When I come unto the children of Israel, and shall say unto them, The God of your fathers hath sent me unto you; and they shall say to me, What is his name? what shall I say unto them?" (Ex. 3:13.)

Perhaps after such long exposure to the idolatry and ways of the Egyptians, and after encountering the dozens of foreign gods of the cultures Egypt traded with, the memory of the true god and his name had become dim. Whatever the reason, when Moses mentioned the name of God, the Israelites would know that Moses did not represent one of the many gods they had heard of. In fact, the name of God would become a memorial to all generations that followed: "God said unto Moses, I AM THAT I AM: and he said, Thus shalt thou say unto the children of Israel, I AM hath sent me unto you. . . . The Lord God of your fathers, the God of Abraham, the God of Isaac, and the God of Jacob, hath sent me unto you: this is my name for ever, and this is my memorial unto all generations." (Ex. 3:14–15.)

The Bible, indeed, is consistent in using the names of God to identify God to the people and to bring him and some aspect of his godhood to remembrance. In his marvelous prophecy of the future Messiah, Isaiah was not content to just declare that he would be born, but he also told us what his name would be: "His name shall be called Wonderful, Counsellor, The mighty God, The everlasting Father, The Prince of Peace." (Isa. 9:6.) By these names, we would recognize the Messiah and know his greatness. Following are some of the names by which we should know Jesus Christ. Each reminds us of a facet of the godhood Jesus possesses:

Symbolic Titles of Jesus Christ

1. The Lord (1 Ne. 1:1)
2. The Lord of Hosts (2 Ne. 8:15)
3. The Lamb (John 1:29)
4. The Light (John 1:7, 8)
5. The Anointed One (Acts 4:27)
6. The Prophet (Deut. 18:15)
7. The Advocate (D&C 45:3–5)
8. The Governor (Matt. 2:6)
9. The King (Matt. 27:42)
10. The King of Glory (Ps. 24:7–8)
11. The Great Creator (2 Ne. 9:5–6)
12. God with Us (Matt. 1:23)
13. The Comforter (John 14:16)
14. The Word (John 1:14)
15. The Rock (Deut. 32:4; 1 Cor. 10:1–4)
16. The Good Shepherd (John 10:11, 14)
17. The True Vine (John 15:1–5)
18. The Lion of Judah (Rev. 5:5)

19. The Door (John 10:7, 9)
20. The Root of David (Rev. 5:5)
21. Only Begotten (Moses 1:6, 21)
22. The Son of God (Heb. 10:29)
23. The Way (John 14:6)
24. The Chief Cornerstone (Eph. 2:20)
25. The Stone of Stumbling (1 Pet. 2:8)
26. The Stumblingblock (1 Cor. 1:23)
27. The Messenger of the Covenant (Mal. 3:1)
28. The Mediator (D&C 107:19)
29. I Am (John 8:58)
30. The Great I Am (D&C 39:1)
31. The Life (John 14:6)
32. He Who Treads the Winepress (D&C 133:50)
33. A Consuming Fire (Heb. 12:29)
34. The Amen (Rev. 3:14)
35. The Living Bread (John 6:51)
36. The High Priest (Heb. 3:1)
37. The Bright and Morning Star (Rev. 22:16)
38. The Bridegroom (D&C 33:17)
39. The Prince of Life (Acts 3:15)
40. The Judge (Gen. 18:25; Acts 10:42)
41. The Deliverer (Rom. 11:26)
42. The Power (1 Cor. 1:24)
43. The Redeemer (D&C 8:1)
44. The Savior (1 Ne. 10:4)
45. Our Passover (1 Cor. 5:7)
46. The Head of Every Man (1 Cor. 11:3)
47. The Captain (Heb. 2:10)
48. Our Peace (Eph. 2:14)
49. The Foundation (1 Cor. 3:11)
50. The Author of Our Faith (Heb. 12:2)
51. Alpha and Omega (D&C 19:1)
52. The Beginning (D&C 35:1)

53. The End (D&C 35:1)
54. The Faithful Witness (Rev. 1:5)
55. The Resurrection (John 11:25)
56. The Truth (John 14:6)
57. The Seed of Abraham (Gal. 3:16)
58. The Physician (Luke 5:31)
59. The Mother Hen (Matt. 23:37)
60. Our Propitiation (Mercy Seat) (Rom. 3:25)
61. The Potter (Jer. 18:6)
62. The Rock of Offense (Rom. 9:33)
63. The Mighty One of Israel (1 Ne. 22:12)
64. The Holy One of Israel (2 Ne. 9:12)

Symbolic Titles Associated with the Events of the Savior's Birth

1. He who is the *Prince of Life* (Acts 3:15) and the source of all life (D&C 88:13) was born in the spring (D&C 20:1), when all life is renewed.

2. He who is the *New David* (Jer. 23:5–6) and the *Root of David* (Rev. 5:5) was born in Bethlehem, which was the city of David (Luke 2:4).

3. He who is the *Lion of the Tribe of Judah* (Rev. 5:5) was born in Judea (Luke 2:4), ancestral homeland of the tribe of Judah.

4. He who is the *Bread of Life* (John 6:48) was born in the city of Bethlehem (Luke 2:4), which in Hebrew means "the house of bread."

5. He who is the *Lamb of God* (John 1:29) was born during Passover season (D&C 20:1) when the Paschal lambs were being offered (Ex. 12:3–6).

6. He who is the *Lamb of God* (John 1:29) was born in a stable (Luke 2:7).

7. He who is the *Good Shepherd* (John 10:14) had his birth first announced to shepherds in the fields (Luke 2:8).

8. He who took upon himself the form of *a Servant* (Philip. 2:7) was born into the humblest of circumstances (Luke 2:7).

9. At the birth of him who is *the Light of the World* (John 8:12), darkness was banished as a sign of his birth (3 Ne. 1:15, 19).

10. At the birth of the *Bright and Morning Star* (Rev. 22:16), a new star appeared as a sign of his birth (Matt. 2:2, 9; 3 Ne. 1:21).

11. At the birth of the *Savior* (Acts 13:23), those who were facing death because they believed on his name, were saved (3 Ne. 1:4–18).

12. He who is called the *King of Kings* (Rev. 19:16) and the *Governor that shall rule Israel* (Matt. 2:6) was greeted by visiting magi and given gifts as though he were a king (Matt. 2:11).

Chapter 8

"The Way Is Prepared from the Fall of Man, and Salvation Is Free"

(2 Nephi 2:4)

One of the most misunderstood and misinterpreted doctrines in all of Christianity is the doctrine of the Fall of Adam. Elder James E. Talmage said, "It has become a common practise with mankind to heap reproaches on the progenitors of the family, and to picture the supposedly blessed state in which we would be living but for the fall; whereas our first parents are entitled to our deepest gratitude for their legacy to posterity—the means of winning title to glory, exaltation, and eternal lives."[1]

The Latter-day Saint conception of the Fall as a necessary part of the overall plan of redemption stems heavily from the doctrines taught in the Book of Mormon. Probably no one taught that doctrine more clearly and forcefully than did father Lehi to Jacob, his firstborn son in the wilderness. Lehi called his posterity together, possibly just shortly before his death, along with the posterity of Ishmael, and gave them his final blessing. Each family group in turn received counsel and admonitions from the great patriarch. (See 2 Nephi 1–4.) Oddly enough, the longest of all of these blessings, as recorded by Nephi, is that given to Jacob. And while the others are more like fatherly admonitions and counsel, Jacob's is a major doctrinal exposition.

Lehi's Discussion of the Fall

Lehi's great blessing to his son is so full of doctrine and meaning that virtually every sentence and, in some cases, every word has significance. Thus, first stepping back and examining the overall picture of what Lehi was trying to do would be helpful. In broad terms, he did four things after his introduction: (1) he outlined five fundamental principles that we must adhere to before we can understand the Fall; (2) he discussed the redemption of the Messiah and how the Messiah can redeem men from the Fall; (3) he discussed the Fall in some detail, particularly focusing on why there had to be a fall; and (4) he concluded by exhorting both Jacob and the other members of his family to wisely use their agency and reap the blessings of the Atonement.

In more detail, the outline of these four points is as follows:

I. FIVE FUNDAMENTALS. (2 Ne. 2:4–5.)
- A. The Spirit is the same yesterday, today, and forever. (V. 4.)
- B. The way is prepared from the fall of man.
- C. Salvation is free.
- D. Men are instructed sufficiently to know good from evil; that is, the law is given unto them. (V. 5.)
- E. By the law, no flesh is justified.
  1. By the temporal law, men are cut off.
  2. By the spiritual law, they perish and become miserable forever.

II. REDEMPTION COMETH IN AND THROUGH THE HOLY MESSIAH. (2 Ne. 2:6–10.)

A. The Messiah:
   1. is full of grace and truth. (V. 6.)
   2. offers himself as a sacrifice for sin.
      a. This answers the ends of the law for those with a broken heart and a contrite spirit. (V. 7.)
      b. Unto none else can the ends of the law be answered.

B. Therefore, no flesh can dwell in God's presence except through his merits, mercy, and grace. (V. 8.)
   1. This is so because he:
      a. laid down his life according to the flesh.
      b. took it up again by the power of the Spirit.
      c. brought resurrection to pass.
   2. These things make him the first fruits unto God and allow him to make intercession for all men. (V. 9.)
   3. This intercession brings all men into God's presence where they:
      a. are judged of him.
      b. receive punishment or happiness. (V. 10.)

III. WHY THE FALL? (2 Ne. 2:11–26.)

A. There must be opposition in all things. (V. 11.) If there weren't:
   1. there could be no righteousness or wickedness, no joy or sorrow, and so on.
   2. all things would be a compound in one.
   3. there would be no death, no life, no mental functions.
   4. there would be no purpose in the creation. (V. 12.)

B. If that were true, then:
   1. God's purposes would be destroyed. (Vv. 12–13.)
   2. it would prove that there is no creation and that we do not exist.

C. But we do exist and there is a God, and he created opposition and gave us agency. (V. 14.)
D. The Fall was part of God's divine plan. To bring about his eternal purposes, God:
   1. set up opposing choices in the Garden of Eden. (V. 15.)
   2. gave man his agency. (V. 16.)
   3. made both choices enticing.
   4. allowed Satan to become the enticer for evil. (Vv. 17–18.)
E. And so Adam and Eve fell. (V. 19.)
   1. They were driven out of the Garden of Eden.
   2. All mankind are born under the effects of the Fall. (V. 20.)
F. The lives of men were prolonged so that they could repent. Mortality became a time of probation. (V. 21.)
   1. Everyone is lost because of the Fall, so everyone must repent.
   2. If there had been no fall:
      a. Adam and Eve would have remained in the Garden of Eden. (V. 22.)
      b. all things would have remained in the same state forever.
      c. Adam and Eve would have had no children. (V. 23.)
      d. Adam and Eve would have remained in a state of innocence, knowing neither good nor evil.
G. Thus we see that the Fall (and all things associated with it) was a reflection of God's wisdom. (V. 25.)
   1. Adam fell so men could be.
   2. Men are, that they might have joy.
   3. The Messiah redeems men from the Fall. (V. 26.)
   4. This allows them to be free and to act for themselves.

IV. LEHI'S EXHORTATION AND SUMMARY. (2 Ne. 2:27–30.)

- A. Two fundamental facts of existence:
  1. men are free according to the flesh. (V. 27.)
  2. all that is expedient is given to them.
- B. The choice is simple. We can choose:
  1. the Mediator, who brings liberty and eternal life.
  2. the Devil, who brings captivity and death.
- C. Lehi earnestly exhorts his sons to (v. 28):
  1. follow the will of the Spirit and choose eternal life by:
     - a. looking to the Mediator.
     - b. hearkening to his commandments.
     - c. being faithful to his words.
  2. not follow the will of the flesh and choose eternal death, because this (v. 29):
     - a. gives the devil power over us.
     - b. brings us down to hell where Satan rules.
- D. Final testimony that Lehi has chosen the good part. (V. 30.)

Let us now examine in more detail what Lehi taught to Jacob.

The Five Fundamentals

In the beginning of his blessing to Jacob, Lehi gave five fundamentals that must be understood before he could go on to discuss the fall and the redemption of man.

Fundamental 1: "The Spirit is the same, yesterday, today, and forever." (V. 4.) This a significant point, especially for Jacob who lived six centuries before the Messiah came to earth to work out the infinite atonement. From this statement of Lehi, we know that the Atonement is bidirectional. That is, it doesn't matter whether one was born prior to the Savior's coming to the earth or afterwards. One can either look forward or backward to the Atonement and have its redemptive power work in his or her behalf.

Indeed, we learn from other sources that the Atonement is not only bidirectional but literally omnidirectional. In Moses 1:33, for example, we are told that by the Only Begotten Son "worlds without number" were created. Elder Bruce R. McConkie, commenting on that verse, said, "Now our Lord's jurisdiction and power extend far beyond the limits of this one small earth on which we dwell. He is, under the Father, the creator of worlds without number (Moses 1:33) and . . . the atonement of Christ, being literally and truly infinite, applies to an infinite number of earths."[2]

Speaking in the same vein, President Marion G. Romney said, "Jesus Christ, is the Lord of the whole universe. Except for his mortal ministry accomplished on this earth, his service and relationship to other worlds and their inhabitants are the same as his service and relationship to this earth and its inhabitants."[3] So, whether we are on this earth or another, in this time or a previous, God is the same yesterday, today, and forever, and the plan of redemption is the same yesterday, today, and forever.

Fundamental 2: "The way is prepared from the fall of man." (2 Ne. 2:4.) Many places in the scriptures clearly teach that the plan of redemption was prepared long before the Fall. (See, for example, D&C 124:33, 41; 128:5; 130:20.) This was Lehi's way of reminding his son of a second foundational principle: that the plan to redeem men from the Fall was laid from the very beginning. In other words, when Adam fell, there was no mad scramble in heaven to determine what to do to save men from the effects of the Fall.

Fundamental 3: "Salvation is free." (2 Ne. 2:4.) Though Lehi gave this statement in three simple words, the concept is profound and important. The best single commentary we have on 2 Nephi 2 is 2 Nephi 9. A careful reading of chapter nine shows that this was *Jacob's own commentary* on the doctrine taught by his father in chapter two. Of particular interest is Jacob's commentary on the concept that salvation is free: "Come, my brethren, every one that thirsteth, come ye to the waters; and he that hath no money, come buy and eat; yea, come buy wine and milk without money and without price. Wherefore, do not spend money for that which is of no worth, nor your labor for that which cannot satisfy." (Vv. 50–51.)

Fundamental 4: "Men are instructed sufficiently that they know good from evil. And the law is given unto men." (2 Ne. 2:5.) In the two foregoing sentences, Lehi stated a fundamental principle in two different ways. Lehi was speaking of those who reach accountability, though he did not explicitly state so. Jacob later made this point clearly. (See 2 Ne. 9:25–26.)

Exactly what did Lehi mean when he said, "Men are instructed sufficiently that they know good from evil" and "The law is given unto men"? We know from other places in scripture that the medium or the means by which this instruction comes to all men is known as the Light of Christ. Through and by the Light of Christ, individuals come to a basic level of understanding of good and evil. Moroni, citing the words of his father, Mormon, said, "The Spirit of Christ is given to every man, that he may know good from evil; wherefore, I show unto you the way to judge; for every thing which inviteth to do good, and to persuade to believe in Christ, is sent forth by the power and gift of Christ; wherefore ye may know with a perfect knowledge it is of God." (Moro. 7:16.)

In latter-day revelation, it was revealed to the Prophet Joseph that this "Spirit of Christ" is also known as "the Light of Christ." (D&C 88:7.) This light is the power that lights the moon and the stars and the sun, the light that gives life to all things and through which all things are governed. (See D&C 88:7–13.)

Fundamental 5: "By the law no flesh is justified." (2 Ne. 2:5.) In that simple statement lies the primary reason why there must be a Redeemer, and so examining Lehi's fifth fundamental at greater length is essential.

The word *justified* and its cognate forms *justification, justice,* or *just* all have the same basic root meaning. To be "just" means to be right or be in order with God. Therefore to be justified (the process of justification) is defined as the "declaration of right, thus judicial acquittal, the opposite of condemnation. . . . Justification may be defined, in its theological sense, as the nonimputation of sin and the imputation of righteousness."[4]

To understand why Lehi said that, by the law, no flesh is justified or that, because of the law, men are cut off, we must first understand the operations of the law of justice. In the Book of Mormon, King Mosiah, Alma, and other prophets discuss this concept of justice in some detail. The law of justice could be simply stated in both its negative and positive forms as follows: (1) for every obedience to the law, there is a blessing; (2) for every violation of the law, there is a punishment (see D&C 130:20–21). The scriptures also clarify that the ultimate blessing coming from obedience to the law is joy and that the punishment coming from violation of the law is misery or suffering. (See, for example, 2 Nephi 2:5.)

Why was it, then, that Lehi said that *no* flesh is justified by the law? Because no one keeps the law perfectly! If the law of justice were the only thing operating, no one could be justified (declared to be right or just) by virtue of the law alone, because as Paul said, "All have sinned, and come short of the glory of God." (Rom. 3:23; see also Rom. 5:12; 1 Ne. 10:6.) So by the law, that is, speaking as though nothing operated but the law itself, men would be cut off both temporally and spiritually. They would be cut off temporally because they do not keep the law perfectly; and they would be cut off spiritually because violation of the law makes one unclean, and "no unclean thing can dwell . . . in his presence." (Moses 6:57; see also 2 Ne. 9:6–10.)

Redemption Cometh in and through the Holy Messiah

Once Lehi laid down the fundamental principles, he turned to what could be thought of as a sixth fundamental principle. But because this principle or truth is of such transcendent importance, he set it apart and discussed it at great length. Second Nephi 2:6, wherein Lehi said, "Wherefore, redemption cometh in and through the Holy Messiah," is the natural follow through from verse five. Simply put, Lehi stated that men are *condemned* by the law but *redeemed* by the Messiah. His qualifying statement about the Messiah—"for he is full of grace and truth"—is interesting in and of itself. In the LDS Bible Dictionary, the following definition is given under the entry "Grace":

> A word that occurs frequently in the New Testament, especially in the writings of Paul. The main idea of the word is *divine means of help or strength,* given through the bounteous mercy and love of Jesus Christ. . . . This grace is an *enabling power* that allows men and women to lay hold on eternal life and exaltation after they have expended their own best efforts. Divine grace is needed by every soul in consequence of the fall of Adam and also because of man's weaknesses and shortcomings.[5]

Lehi's point was that, if Christ were not full of this grace or this "enabling power," the redemption would not be possible.

Lehi's next statement was that the Holy Messiah would offer himself as "a sacrifice for sin, to answer the ends of the law." (2 Ne. 2:7.) In light of our understanding of the law of justice, we see why Lehi made this statement. Remembering the two principles that constitute the law of justice, i.e. obedience brings joy, violation brings suffering, one could say that there are only two ways to satisfy the demands of that law. The *first* would be to keep the law perfectly; that is, to never violate in any degree the law that is given. The second way would be to pay the penalty for any violations.

This is what the Messiah did, for he met both conditions. Jesus kept the law perfectly. Not once in his entire mortal life did he violate the law in any degree or in any way. He was the Lamb without spot or blemish. He was the ultimate in perfection. Here then was one who, in Lehi's words, was justified by the law. In other words, the law had no claim on him. But Christ did more than this. In 2 Nephi 9:21, Jacob again added commentary to our understanding of what his father taught: the Messiah "suffereth the pains of all men, yea, the pains of every living creature, both men, women, and children, who belong to the family of Adam." So not only did Christ keep the law perfectly for himself, but he suffered the penalty for all violations as though he himself were guilty of them.

Lehi indicated that the sacrifice answering the ends of the law was given only for those who have "a broken heart and a contrite spirit." Then he added, "unto *none else*" can that be done. (2 Ne. 2:7.) To better understand why Lehi made this statement and what it fully means for us, let us examine the doctrine of grace and works.

Members of the Church, particularly missionaries, have often been called upon to defend the belief that the way people live (or their works) plays a critical role in their salvation. Protestants, especially evangelical Christians, cite several references from Paul's writings to indicate that a man is saved by grace. (See Acts 16:31; Rom. 3:28; 10:13; Gal. 2:16;

Grace and Works — One Explanation

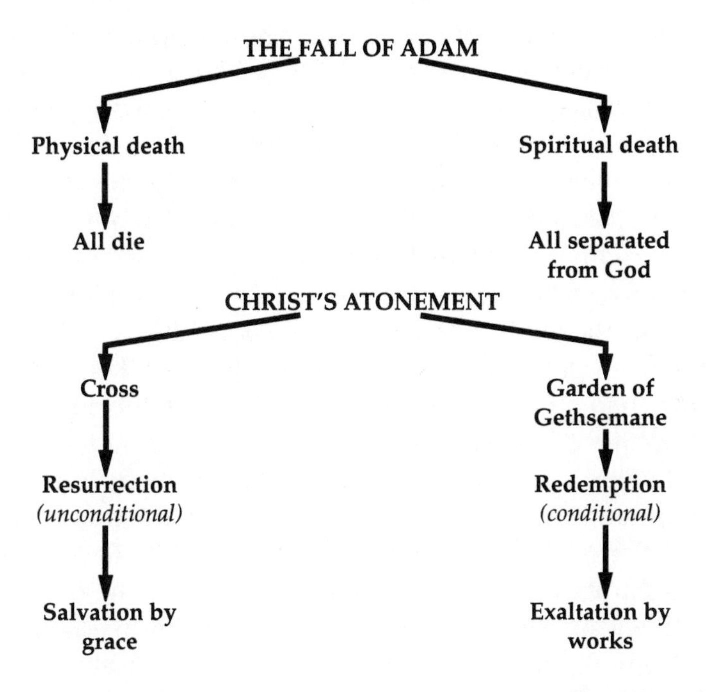

Eph. 2:8–9.) Those statements by Paul have created some awkwardness in the minds of some Latter-day Saints, especially missionaries, about the issue of salvation by grace. The above diagram, though faulty, has been used by some to help answer those questions.

Those using this diagram explain it by saying that through the Fall of Adam there were two deaths that came upon mankind. One is physical death, which is the separation of the body and the spirit. All of Adam and Eve's posterity are subject to mortality and will die. But there is also a spiritual death. This is defined as being cut off or separated from the presence of God. Because Adam and Eve were cast out of the Garden of Eden, all men are born in a state of separation from the presence of God, or in a state of spiritual death.

The diagram goes on to show how Christ's redemption covers both aspects of the Fall. On the cross, the Savior gave up his life but then took it up again, thus overcoming physical death and providing the resurrection. Since no one has to do anything to be resurrected, one could say that this is an unconditional blessing. This explains how we are "saved by grace" without any works on our part. We need do nothing; the grace of Christ resurrects everyone.

But, the explanation continues, there is a second part of the redemption that cannot be overlooked. This part was done in the Garden of Gethsemane. Here the Savior took upon himself the sins of the world and suffered for all mankind. This suffering provided the redemption, but this redemption is *not* unconditional. Here men must do things to have the redemption operate in their behalf. This could be thought of as exaltation by our works. Thus, the conclusion runs, we are saved (resurrected) by grace, but we are exalted (redeemed) by our works. This is a neat and attractive explanation. *The only difficulty is that it has four major doctrinal problems.*

The first doctrinal problem in this explanation is assuming that salvation is different from exaltation. With very few exceptions, the scriptures almost always use the words *salvation* and *exaltation* synonymously. For example, in Doctrine and Covenants 6:13, the Lord says, "If thou wilt do good, yea, and hold out faithful to the end, thou shalt be *saved* in the kingdom of God, which is the greatest of all the gifts of God; for there is no gift greater than the gift of *salvation*." (Italics added.) Resurrection, wonderful as it is, is not the greatest gift of God; eternal life, or exaltation, is. (See D&C 14:7.) To imply that salvation means only resurrection cannot be supported by scripture.

The second doctrinal problem is the idea that the cross covered only the effects of physical death and that the suffering in the Garden covered only the effects of spiritual death. Such an explanation is not justified by scripture either. The agony in the Garden and the suffering on the cross were both integral parts of the atoning sacrifice. Nowhere do we find indications that the cross alone overcame physical death or that the Garden alone overcame spiritual death.

The third problem is the idea that our works exalt us. As we have seen, one of Lehi's fundamental points is that no man can be justified, or saved, on the basis of works alone. Only by the merits, mercy, and grace of the Holy Messiah (see 2 Ne. 2:8) are we saved. Righteous works *do* exalt us, but *they are the Savior's works,* not our own (by the simple fact that we cannot fully satisfy the law by our works alone). This is what Nephi meant when he said, "For we know that it is by grace [which quality the Messiah is filled with—see 2 Ne. 2:6] that we are saved, after all we can do." (2 Ne. 25:23.)

The fourth problem is the idea that overcoming that part of spiritual death (which resulted from the fall of Adam) is conditional upon how we live. Our second Article of Faith states, "We believe that men will be punished for their own sins, and not for Adam's transgression." To make coming back into the presence of God (overcoming spiritual death) conditional, when the fall of Adam originally caused our separation from him, would mean we suffer punishment for Adam's transgression; and such is not the case. Let us now redo the chart so that it reflects not only what father Lehi taught, but what the other scriptures also teach.

The upper part of the previous chart is correct. The fall of Adam did bring two deaths into the world—physical death and spiritual death. But so far as it applies to Adam's fall, Christ's redemption is unconditional and applies to all. In other words, since we did nothing to be under the effects of

The Messiah Redeems Men from the Fall

("We believe that men will be punished for their own sins"—A of F 2)

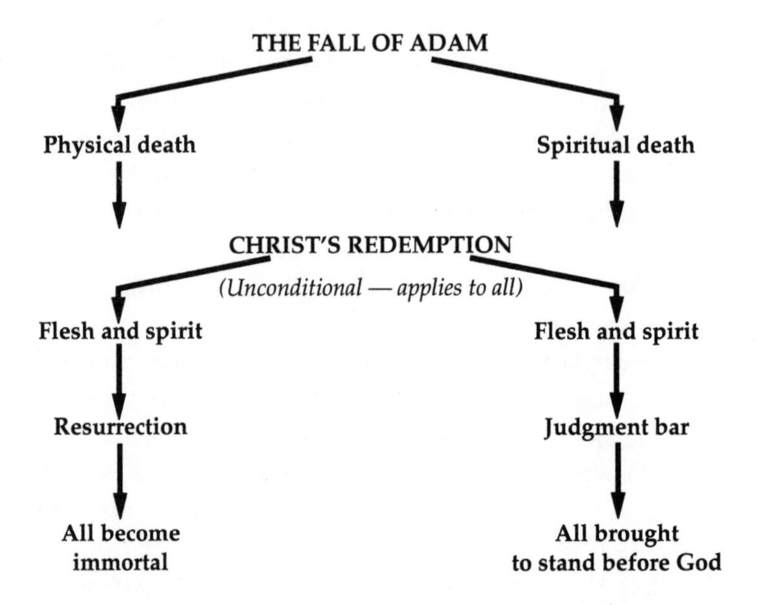

the Fall, except come through the lineage of Adam, it is not fair (or just) that we should have to meet any conditions in order to have those effects taken from us.

In 2 Nephi 2:8, Lehi said, "[He] layeth down his life according to the flesh, and taketh it again by the power of the Spirit." Lehi mentioned both the suffering of the flesh and the suffering of the spirit as necessary to bring about the resurrection of the dead. This resurrection is unconditional, and all become immortal. But in verse ten, Lehi went further and said, "Because of the intercession for all, *all men come unto God;* wherefore, *they stand in the presence of him,* to be judged of him according to the truth and holiness which is in him." (Italics added.)

That is a pivotal point. Not only does Christ's redemption bring about resurrection for all without condition, it also brings all men to the judgment bar where they are brought into the presence of the Lord to be judged. If we are brought back into the presence of God, then spiritual death, or the separation from God that came because of Adam's fall, is at that point overcome. What does a person have to do to have this happen? Absolutely nothing. It is unconditional. Thus the Savior automatically redeems us from both effects of the fall of Adam.

The Fall of Me

Now, however, we must consider Lehi's fourth fundamental point. As he said, "Men are instructed sufficiently that they know good from evil." (2 Ne. 2:5.) If we know good from evil and then sin (which, according to Paul, all men do), then we must talk about a second fall. This is not the fall of Adam. This is *one's own personal fall.* This fall, which our own, not Adam's, transgression brings about, requires redemption as surely as mankind needed redemption from the consequences of Adam's fall. We'll term this the "fall of me." The diagram on the following page charts what happens as the result of the "fall of me."

Once a person reaches the age of accountability and sins through the use of his agency, he becomes unclean. Unless something happens, when he is brought back into God's presence at the judgment, he will not be allowed to stay. Now, since we have no one to blame for this except ourselves, our redemption becomes conditional upon our actions. This is what Lehi meant when he said that the sacrifice that the Messiah offered to satisfy the ends of the law is viable only for those with a broken heart and a contrite spirit. This con-

He Offereth Himself unto Those with a Broken Heart

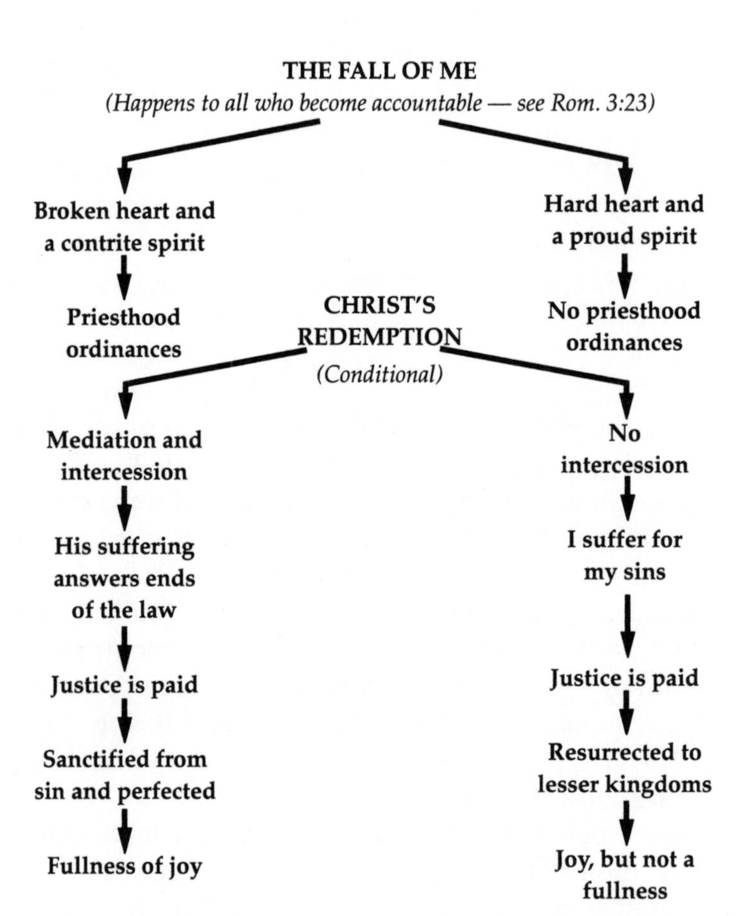

dition, which comes through faith and godly sorrow (see 2 Cor. 7:9–10)—or in other words, repentance—brings one to participate in the redemptive ordinances: baptism, confirmation, receiving the priesthood, and the temple ordinances.

Those who refuse to make this new sacrifice (see 3 Ne.

9:20) are characterized in the scriptures as having a hard heart and a proud spirit. These are conditions that lead one to reject the priesthood ordinances. These conditions may also exist, in some cases, even though the outward ordinances may have been performed. In other words, some members of the Church who have been baptized and confirmed, who have received the Holy Ghost and perhaps even temple ordinances, have not exhibited broken hearts and contrite spirits. They go through the outward motions only and therefore experience no validity in those ordinances, no saving power.

What happens, though, to a person who does meet the conditions of a broken heart and a contrite spirit? The left side of the diagram shows the process. The words Lehi used are "mediation" and "intercession." (2 Ne. 2:9–10, 27.) The Messiah's mediation and intercession are applied to those with broken hearts and contrite spirits, and his suffering, both on the cross and in the Garden, and his perfect obedience to law answer the demands of the law of justice. Or in Lehi's words, his life and death serve as a "sacrifice for sin." (V. 7.) The demands of the law are thus met; in other words, justice is paid not robbed. (See Alma 42:25.) The person is sanctified from sin and perfected.

Lehi's statement that the Messiah's merits and not our own merits save us is beautifully supported in the Doctrine and Covenants, wherein the Son says:

> Listen to him who is the advocate with the Father, who is pleading your cause before him—saying: Father, *behold the sufferings and death of him who did no sin,* in whom thou wast well pleased; behold the blood of thy Son which was shed, the blood of him whom thou gavest that thyself might be glorified; wherefore, Father, spare these my brethren that believe on my name, that they may come unto me and have everlasting life. (D&C 45:3–5; italics added.)

What happens, then, to those who do not meet the basic

conditions of having a broken heart and a contrite spirit? The right side of the diagram illustrates this. For those hard of heart and proud of spirit who refuse to accept redemptive ordinances, Christ's redemption becomes inoperative. He does not make intercession in their behalf, and he clearly explains so in a modern revelation:

> Surely every man must repent or suffer. . . . Therefore I command you to repent—repent, lest I smite you by the rod of my mouth, and by my wrath, and by my anger, and your sufferings be sore—how sore you know not . . . For behold, I, God, have suffered these things for all, that they might not suffer if they would repent; *but if they would not repent they must suffer even as I.* (D&C 19:4, 15–17, italics added.)

Either way, justice is paid. The price of suffering is met. But whereas the Messiah's atoning sacrifice paid the price for the humble and obedient, the rest must pay the price themselves. And how much is that price we would pay ourselves? We don't know exactly, but the Lord described his own suffering: "Which suffering caused myself, even God, the greatest of all, to tremble because of pain, and to bleed at every pore, and to suffer both body and spirit—and would that I might not drink the bitter cup, and shrink." (D&C 19:18.) No wonder he commands, "Confess your sins, lest you suffer these punishments of which I have spoken" (D&C 19:20), and urges us to "preach naught but repentance" (D&C 19:21) so that others would not suffer as he did.

Why the Fall?

After laying the foundational principles firmly in place, Lehi was ready to turn his attention to the question of the Fall and why it had to happen. Not surprisingly, the Fall has caused a great deal of confusion and misinterpretation, for on the surface it raises some difficult questions. Though Lehi did not pose these questions openly, he seemed to sense them and proceeded to answer them with a marvelous chain of logical reasoning. Lehi's linchpin argument in explaining why the Fall was necessary is summarized in the well-known scripture "For it must needs be, that there is an opposition in all things." (2 Ne. 2:11.) How pivotal this is to Lehi's whole line of reasoning in this chapter can be seen from how much time—verses eleven through fifteen—he spends defending and explaining that statement. Lehi used an interesting chain of reasoning to substantiate his statement. If it were put into a diagram, it would look something like this:

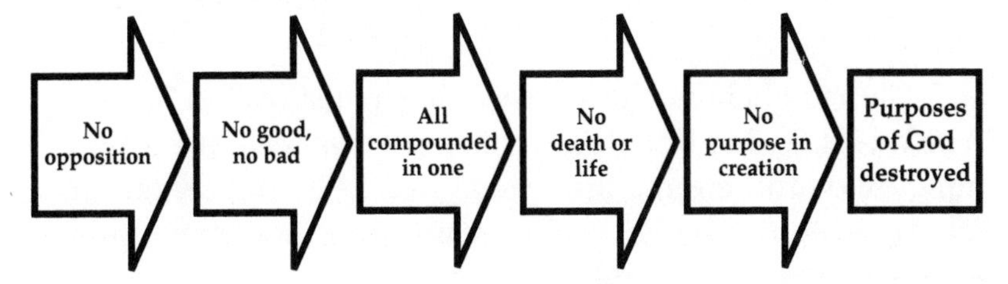

In Moses 1:39, we learn that God's purposes have to do with bringing to pass the immortality and eternal life of man. Therefore, if God's purposes were destroyed, the whole plan of salvation would become meaningless.

Then, as though he had not made his point strongly enough, Lehi started again and put it in other words, reiterating a similar line of reasoning. Again if that were diagramed, it would look like this:

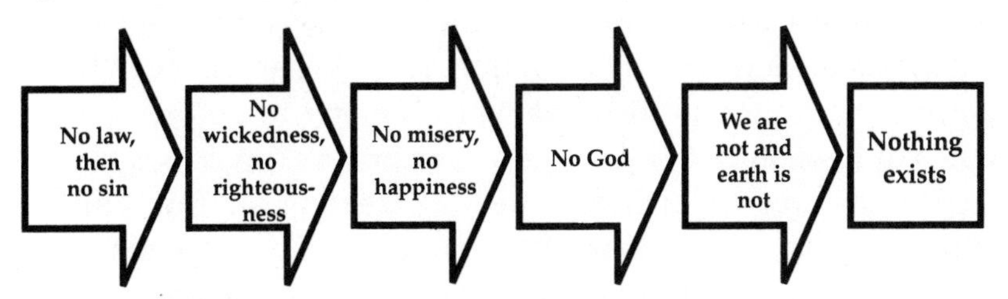

If there is any one thing we can be certain of, it is our own existence. So working backwards from that irrefutable evidence, Lehi showed that God exists and therefore has created all things, and that, as he explained it in 2 Nephi 2:14, includes "both things to act and things to be acted upon."

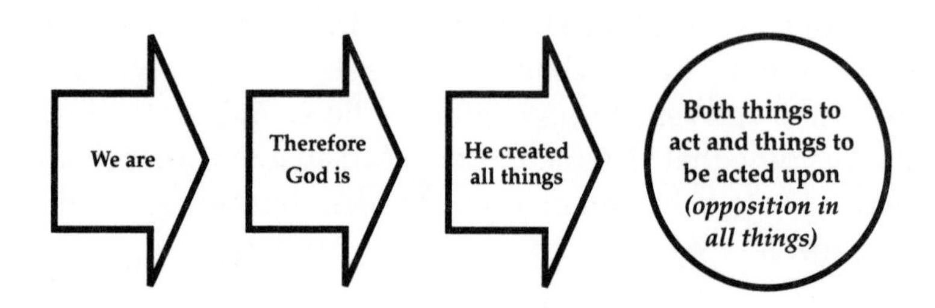

To sum up Lehi's chain of reasoning in just two sentences: In order for God to bring about his purposes with man (their immortality and eternal life), there had to be opposition or opposing alternatives. If there were no opposition, men could not be exalted because there would be no accountability.

This brings us to an important question—if opposition is necessary, why didn't God just create a world of opposition? Here, other scriptures help us understand why this could not be so. Moroni, citing his father's teaching, indicates that "all things which are good cometh of God; and that which is evil cometh of the devil." (Moro. 7:12.)

The Prophet Joseph Smith, in the *Lectures on Faith,* indicated that one of the prerequisites for a man to have faith is to have an understanding of the nature, attributes, and *perfections* of God.[6] He then commented, "What we mean by perfections is, the perfections which belong to all the attributes of his nature."[7] From these and other sources we conclude the three following points: (1) creating anything imperfect or unholy is contrary to the nature of God; (2) enticing men to violate law or to do evil is contrary to the nature of God; and (3) if God had created a world in which there was opposition, sin, and evil, then we could hold him responsible for such conditions.[8]

Therefore, the creation of the world (and man) was done in a perfect, holy, and innocent state. To have done otherwise would have been contrary to the nature of God, which sets up an interesting problem. Opposition is necessary to man's progression, but God could not create it and be true to his perfect nature.

The Fall Was Part of God's Divine Plan

Lehi explained how this dilemma was resolved. Note the following points that he made: (1) In verse fifteen, he indicated that God created our first parents and all things that were created. (2) God set up an opposition from the beginning, even the opposition of the forbidden fruit to the tree of life. (3) In verse sixteen, Lehi indicated that God gave agency unto man. (4) If man were to be truly free to act for himself, or in other words, if there were to be truly opposite choices (or opposition), he must be enticed by those choices. (5) Since God cannot entice man to make bad choices, Satan was allowed to come to earth and entice men to do evil. (See 2 Ne. 2:17–18.) This final point is validated in other latter-day revelation. To the Prophet Joseph Smith, the Lord said:

> It must needs be [note the same language here that Lehi used] that the devil should tempt the children of men, or they could not be agents unto themselves; for if they never should have bitter they could not know the sweet—wherefore, it came to pass that the devil tempted Adam, and he partook of the forbidden fruit and transgressed the commandment. (D&C 29:39–40.)

The positive side of the option given to Adam was clearly enticing in and of itself. The Garden of Eden was a beautiful and alluring place in which to live. Flowers and trees flourished and brought forth fruit spontaneously. There was neither death nor sorrow, nor was there wickedness. But how could the opposite be made enticing so that true opposition could exist? This is why Satan and his angels were cast down to earth and allowed to function.

Lehi made five important points as to why the Fall happened and how the Fall helped the Lord fulfill his divine plan of redemption: (1) opposition is necessary for man's progression (v. 11); (2) the Lord set up opposing choices (v. 15); (3) he gave man his agency (v. 16); (4) in order to make that agency operative, both choices had to be enticing (v. 16; D&C 29:39); and (5) God allowed Satan, who makes the negative option sound as enticing as the positive, to operate in the Garden and in this world.

Once Lehi established why the Fall had to take place, he discussed the results of the Fall for us. He pointed out that, since the Fall had taken place and men were born into the world under the effects of that fall, this life became a state of probation or a time to prove ourselves. He indicated that the days of the children of men were prolonged so they might repent and begin to bring into operation the full plan of redemption. (See 2 Ne. 2:21.) Lehi further emphasized the importance of the Fall by pointing out what would have happened if the Fall had never taken place. (See vv. 22–23.) He stated that Adam and Eve would have remained in the Garden of Eden. In particular, all things that were created would have remained in the state they were in prior to the Fall, which was a state of perfection, innocence, spontaneous multiplication, with no death or sorrow. Also Adam and Even would have had no children. And "they would have remained in a state of innocence, having no joy, for they knew no misery; doing no good, for they knew no sin." (V. 23.)

When one examines the four conditions that resulted from the Fall, it becomes evident that all of these are conditions necessary for the progression of mankind toward Godhood.

They are necessary for man to prove himself and to become accountable before God. Therefore, again noting that, if there had been no fall, the purposes of God would have been frustrated, Lehi concluded: "All things have been done in the wisdom of him who knoweth all things. Adam fell that men might be; and men are, that they might have joy. And the Messiah cometh in the fulness of time, that he may redeem the children of men from the fall." (2 Ne. 2:24–26.)

Lehi's Exhortation

With the fundamental facts laid out and an explanation given as to why the Fall was necessary, Lehi made his final moving exhortation to Jacob and his other sons. (See vv. 27–30.) First, he indicated that men are free according to the flesh and all that is expedient is given unto them. That provides a simple yet profound formula:

freedom (agency) + knowledge = accountability

Without accountability, there could be no sin or punishment. Without accountability, God could not make men gods, for there would be no merit in doing good if there were no other choice than to be good. But God set up both conditions required to have accountability.

Second, Lehi noted that the choice is really simple. As King Benjamin pointed out, there are many ways to commit sin, so many in fact that they cannot be numbered. (See Mosiah 4:29.) But in Lehi's thinking, all choices, all options, all alternatives come down to one basic ultimate choice. It is this: "Men are free according to the flesh; and all things are given them which are expedient unto man. And they are free to choose liberty and eternal life, through the great Mediator of all men, or to choose captivity and death, according to the captivity and power of the devil." (2 Ne. 2:27.)

Third, he exhorted his sons to follow the will of the Spirit and choose eternal life by doing three things: (1) looking to the Mediator, (2) hearkening to his commandments, and (3) being faithful to his words. (See v. 28.) The other alternative is to follow the will of the flesh and choose eternal death, which gives the spirit of the devil power over us and brings us down to hell where Satan rules. (See v. 29.) Finally Lehi closed his blessing to his son Jacob with his own testimony. He said simply, "I have chosen the good part, according to the words of the prophet." (V. 30.)

Elder James E. Talmage had said that it has become common, even among Christians, to heap reproaches upon Adam and Eve for the Fall. But he concluded that we instead owe them a great deal:

> Our first parents are entitled to our deepest gratitude for their legacy to posterity—the means of winning title to glory, exaltation, and eternal lives. But for the opportunity thus given, the spirits of God's offspring would have remained forever in a state of innocent childhood, sinless through no effort of their own; negatively saved, not from sin, but from the opportunity of meeting sin; incapable of winning the honors of victory because prevented from taking part in the conflict. As it is, they are heirs to the birthright of Adam's descendants—mortality, with its immeasurable possibilities and its God-given freedom of action. From Father Adam we have inherited all the ills to which flesh is heir; but such are necessary incident to a knowledge of good and evil, by the proper use of which knowledge man may become even as the Gods.[9]

Lehi's marvelous blessing to his son Jacob provides much of the reason why this is the case. In one couplet, he caught the essence of it all: "'Adam fell that men might be; and men are, that they might have joy." (2 Ne. 2:25.)

Chapter 9

"Even So Ye Must Be Born Again"

(Moses 6:59)

The scriptures often refer to "the doctrine of Christ" (2 Ne. 31:21), which the Savior clearly defined as follows: "The Father commandeth all men, everywhere, to repent and believe in me. And whoso believeth in me, and is baptized, the same shall be saved; and they are they who shall inherit the kingdom of God. And whoso believeth not in me, and is not baptized, shall be damned. Verily, verily, I say unto you, that *this is my doctrine.*" (3 Ne. 11:32–35; italics added.)

The doctrine of Christ is taught in many places in the scriptures (see, for example, 2 Ne. 31:11–21; 32:1–6; 3 Ne. 11:31–40; D&C 10:63–69), but perhaps nowhere was it more fully and clearly taught than in the very beginning to Father Adam. In Moses 6:48–62, this fuller account ties the first principles and ordinances to the fall of Adam and the atoning sacrifice. In other words, it contains a full discussion of the Father's plan. This is why the closing verse clearly states: "And now, behold, I say unto you: *This is the plan of salvation unto all men.*" (V. 62; italics added.)

The flow chart on pages 108–9 is an attempt to help you better conceptualize what is taught in those verses in the book of Moses. Without a careful prereading and constant referral back to the scriptural passages, the chart will not be fully understood. Additional references that help clarify the doctrine are given below some of the boxes on the chart.

It is important to remember that the scriptures, not the chart, contain the reality of these saving truths. The chart is only an instructional device to help you conceptualize those saving truths and doctrines. Only as you immerse yourself in the scriptural sources—carefully, thoughtfully, and prayerfully—will the chart become a meaningful instructional experience.

The analogy of rebirth needs a brief explanation. In Moses 6:59, the Lord indicates that we are born into this world through water, blood, and spirit. In other words, three elements are essential to our birth into mortality. For the first nine months of life, the unborn fetus is totally immersed in the amniotic fluid in the uterus. This watery environment protects the child and allows it to move freely inside the mother. When the "water breaks," the mother knows that birth is imminent. So water is the first essential element.

Blood is the second. The circulatory system develops early in the unborn child. Blood becomes the life-giving and life-sustaining fluid in the tiny new body. Blood has three primary functions: It brings oxygen and food to all parts of the body, it carries carbon dioxide and waste products away, and it protects and fights against infection and disease through the white blood cells.

The third element of our physical birth is the spirit. We are not told exactly when the spirit enters the body, but if the spirit is not present at birth, there will be no life. (See Alma 40:11; D&C 93:33–34.) Such a baby would be called a "stillborn" child.

The Lord, in simple but significant imagery, likens our spiritual rebirth to our birth into mortality. As it was with our first birth, so it is when we are "born again." Water, blood, and Spirit are again essential. In the water of the baptismal font, we are again totally immersed in a watery environment. In other words, the baptismal font is not only a symbol of the grave, where we bury the old sinful man, but also a symbol of the womb where the newborn spiritual person is given life. The atoning blood of Christ is also required, and like the blood in our bodies, the atoning blood nourishes, cleanses, and protects us from spiritual infection. And finally, the source of life for the reborn spiritual man is the Holy Spirit. If it were not so, the newborn spiritual man would be "stillborn."

One other thought: Does not this concept of rebirth give a wider and deeper dimension to the commandment that we "become as a little child" (3 Ne. 11:37–38; see also Mosiah 3:19) if we are to overcome the natural man and become "the children of Christ, his sons, and his daughters" (Mosiah 5:7)? This is the profound and beautiful imagery of being born again through the water, blood, and Spirit.

"The Doctrine of Christ"

(2 Ne. 31:21; see Moses 6:48–62)

Fall of Adam

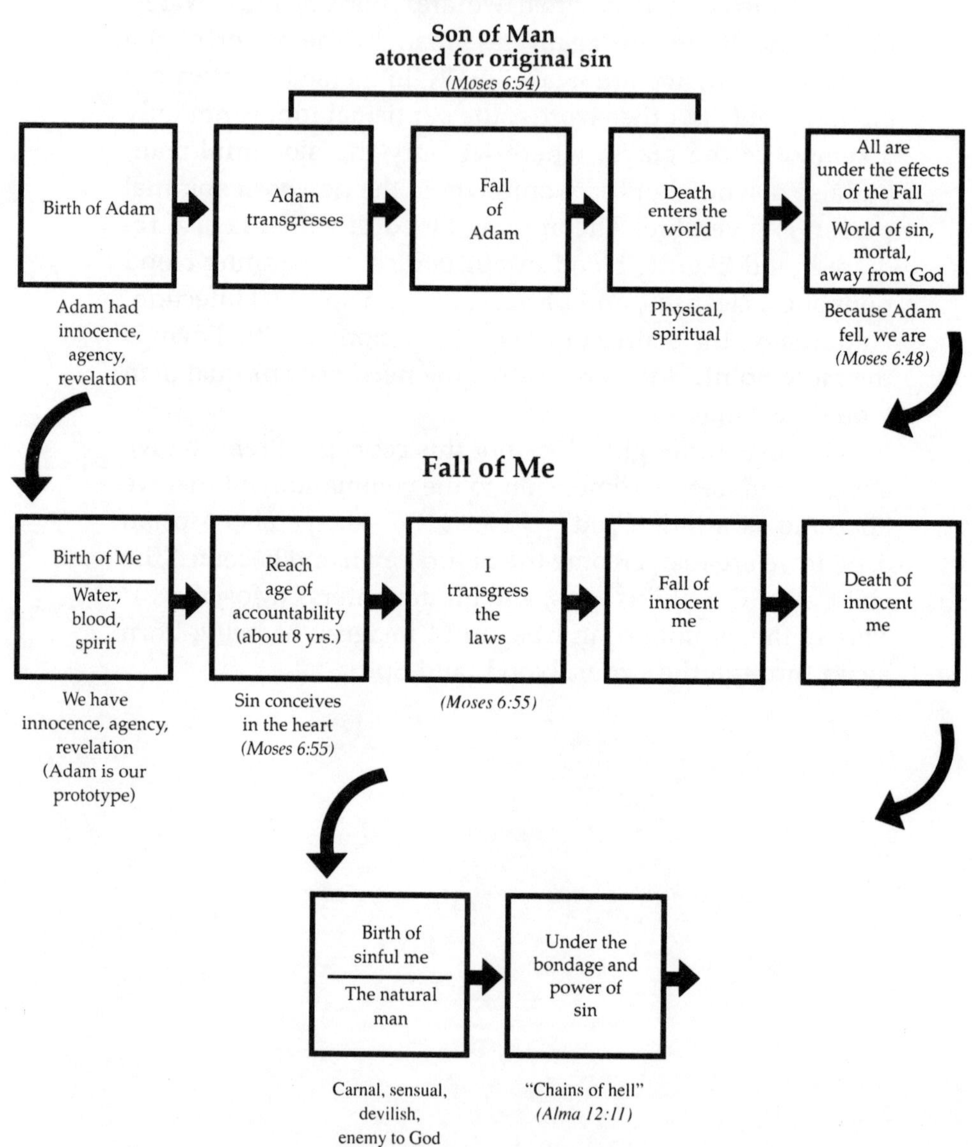

First Principles and Ordinances

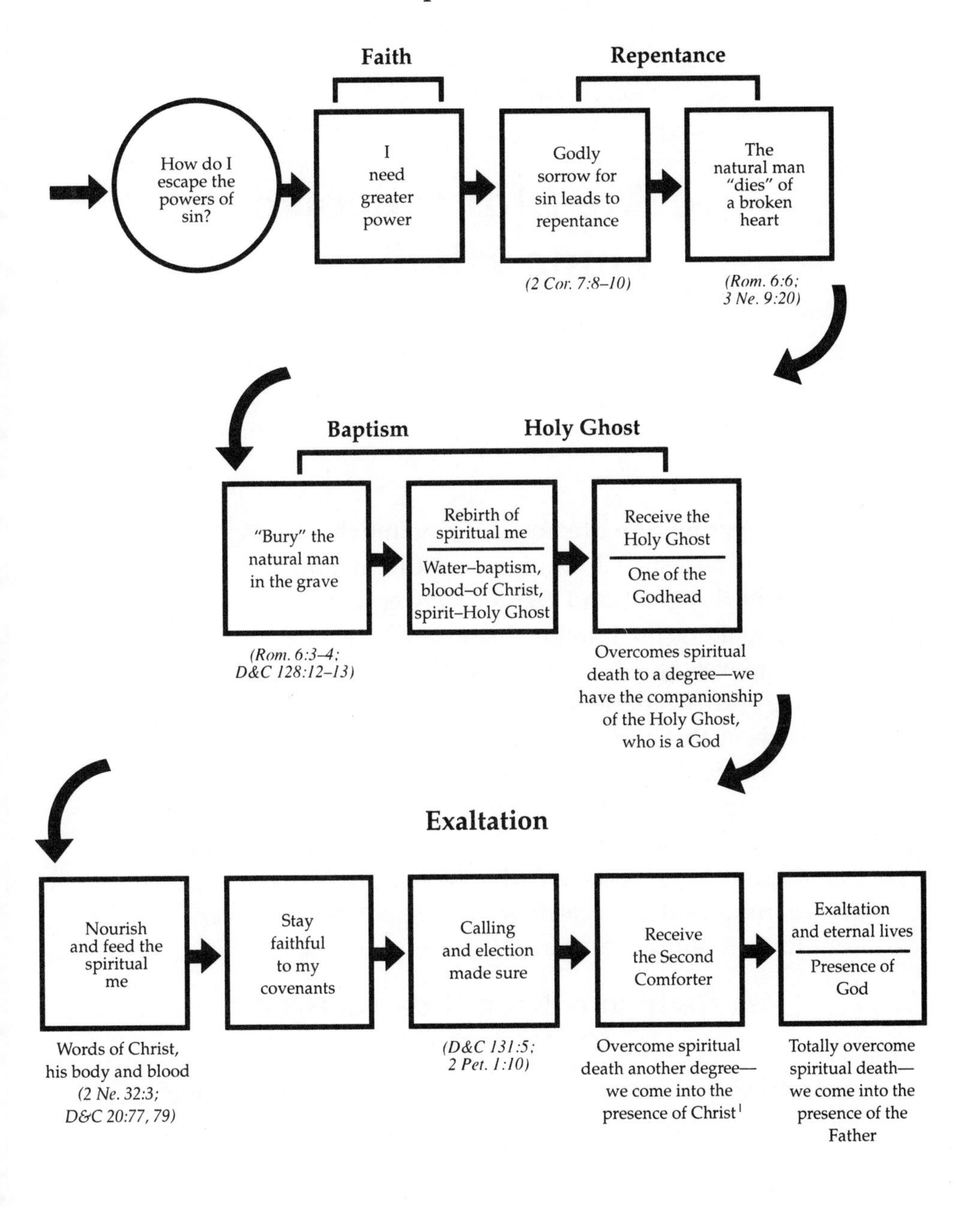

Chapter 10

"Ye Are Still Indebted unto Him"

(Mosiah 2:24)

In preparing to write about divine indebtedness and the atonement of Jesus Christ, I reread the magnificent closing sermon of the great and righteous King Benjamin. I pored over it, looking for relationships, outlining the major concepts, and watching for patterns in King Benjamin's thinking. Because of that experience, I have decided to follow a similar approach in this chapter. I intend to examine the message of the king, look at its antecedents, outline its structure, note relationships within that structure, watch for patterns in the words and phrases he chose to use, and explore some of the implications for us today of what he taught. I wish to let this great sermon speak for itself on the relationship between our debt to God and the atoning sacrifice of our Savior.

A Righteous King Bids Farewell to His People

In order to understand the full impact of King Benjamin's address, we must examine the setting that drew it forth.

Mormon, writing some four centuries later, informed us about King Benjamin and the circumstances that led to his last great sermon. (See W of M 1:12–18; Mosiah 1:1–2:8.) Benjamin did not inherit a comfortable situation when he became the king of the Nephite peoples. It was a time of war, with armies of the Lamanites coming down against the Nephites. King Benjamin led his people in battle, wielding the sword of Laban with his own hand. Thousands were killed, and eventually the Lamanites were driven out of the land. (See W of M 1:13–14.)

But the external threat to the Nephite society was not the only problem. During the kingship before Benjamin's reign, the Nephites had incorporated the Mulekite people, whose language was different and whose knowledge of Jehovah and the Mosaic law had been corrupted. Teaching them a new language and a new religion and having that settle in would have been difficult and time-consuming. (See Omni 1:14–19.) Mormon said that, besides the wars with the Lamanites, there were "contentions among his [Benjamin's] own people." Mormon also explained that there were "false Christs," "false prophets," and "false preachers and teachers" among the people. "Many dissensions" also arose, and the people were described as stiffnecked. (W of M 1:12, 15–17.)

This was the society over which Benjamin ruled, and these were the people he led. Benjamin, however, was not content with that state of affairs. With the assistance of holy prophets, whom he sustained, and through his own personal righteousness, King Benjamin brought a complete turnaround among his people. In two sweeping sentences, Mormon summarized Benjamin's greatness: "King Benjamin, by laboring with all the might of his body and the faculty of his whole soul, . . . did once more establish peace in the land." (W of M 1:18.) "Now there was no more contention in all the land of Zarahemla, among all the people who belonged to king Benjamin, so that king Benjamin had continual peace all the remainder of his days." (Mosiah 1:1.) By "peace," Mormon almost certainly meant here far more than the mere absence of war.

Mormon did not tell us how many years King Benjamin's reign lasted, though it seems to have been a lengthy one (see, for example, Mosiah 2:12, 16, 19), but oh what a reign it must have been! When the people learned that the king was turning the kingdom over to his son, when they heard that this would be the last speech of their beloved king, a vast crowd gathered, as Mormon explained, to

> give thanks to the Lord their God, who had brought them out of the land of Jerusalem, and who had delivered them out of the hands of their enemies, and had appointed just men to be their teachers, and also a just man to be their king, who had established peace in the land of Zarahemla, and who had taught them to keep the commandments of God, that they might rejoice and be filled with love towards God and all men. (Mosiah 2:4.)

There must have been a tremendous outpouring of love and gratitude toward the king. Even Benjamin seemed unprepared for the huge multitudes that responded to the proclamation to come and hear their king. When the multitude spilled out beyond the temple courtyard, a tower was built. But even that was not sufficient, and Benjamin had to have his words written and sent to those who could not hear his voice. (See Mosiah 2:7–8.)

Surely as the throngs came, Benjamin would have been inundated with people seeking to thank him for all that he had done. He must have had a constant stream of people grasping his hand, saying, "Thank you for what you are. Thank you for what you've done for us." Praise and thanks for his goodness and greatness must have rained upon him like a tropical downpour.

Many men might be tempted in the face of such praise to say in their hearts, "Yes, you are right. I have done well." But Benjamin would have none of that. He would not let the credit and praise rest with him. He epitomized the counsel of the apostle Paul to every man "not to think of himself more highly than he ought to think." (Rom. 12:3.) To God went the glory. These were his opening thoughts as he spoke to his people:

> I have not commanded you to come up hither that ye should fear me, or that ye should think that I of myself am more than a mortal man. But I am like as yourselves, subject to all manner of infirmities in body and mind; yet I have been chosen by this people, and consecrated by my father, and was suffered by the hand of the Lord that I should be a ruler and a king over this people; and have been kept and preserved by his matchless power, to serve you with all the might, mind and strength which the Lord hath granted unto me. (Mosiah 2:10–11.)

Benjamin also undoubtedly felt an urgency to deliver a special message, one of great hope and deliverance that an angel had declared to him. The message, he stated, was another reason he had called his people together. Benjamin described this experience thus:

> The things which I shall tell you are made known unto me by an angel from God. And he said unto me: Awake; and I awoke, and behold he stood before me. And he said unto me: . . . I am come to declare unto you the glad tidings of great joy. For the Lord hath heard thy prayers, and hath judged of thy righteousness, and hath sent me to declare unto thee that thou mayest rejoice; and that thou mayest declare unto thy people, that they may also be filled with joy. (Mosiah 3:2–4.)

This, then, is the context from which we must examine King Benjamin's last address to his people, asking ourselves why he would choose a theme of indebtedness to God.

Our Indebtedness to Our Heavenly King (Mosiah 2:18–26)

King Benjamin first gave what might be termed a brief "stewardship report" to the people whom he had served. And what a report that was! We learn that King Benjamin was a man of honor and justice. He had not suffered his people to be placed in prisons or to practice slavery. He had not allowed crime or any kind of wickedness. He had labored with his own hands so as not to lay burdensome taxes on his people, and he had not sought to enrich himself by taking from the people. (See Mosiah 2:12–14.)

How his people must have loved him! Peace, security, honesty, justice, prosperity, righteousness—these were the legacies that he left for them. The long and melancholy history of monarchies clearly testifies how few kings there have been who could give such a stewardship report as this at the end of their earthly reign.

Hastily, lest he be misunderstood, the king noted that this report was not an attempt to boast of his accomplishments, but only an acknowledgment that his service to his people had merely been an extension of his desire to serve God. (See Mosiah 2:16.) Then, in what is surely one of the finest, most beautiful, and most succinct lessons on Christian service ever given, he stated the pivotal lesson of his own righteous life. If ye would learn anything from me, he said, learn this one lesson: "When ye are in the service of your fellow beings ye are only in the service of your God." (Mosiah 2:17.)

King Benjamin's stewardship report and the resulting lesson on service led him naturally to the concept of divine indebtedness. He had already noted that any success he had enjoyed came only through the grace and sustaining power of God. So their praise of him was misdirected. "If I, whom ye call your king," he pointed out, "do merit any thanks from you, O how you ought to thank your heavenly King!" (Mosiah 2:19.) This provided the basis for King Benjamin's concept of divine indebtedness. It is a lesson as applicable today as when given to the Nephites gathered in their tents in the Land of Zarahemla.

A careful look at Mosiah 2:20–25 reveals the structure of King Benjamin's primary thoughts about our indebtedness to God. It would go something like this capsulized into outline form:

I. OUR INDEBTEDNESS TO GOD. (Mosiah 2:20–25.)
- A. God has done the following for Benjamin's people (v. 20):
  1. created them.
  2. kept and preserved them.
  3. caused them to rejoice.
  3. granted that they should have peace.
- B. He continues to:
  1. preserve them day to day by giving them breath. (V. 21.)
  2. allow them to live and to move and to do as they will.
  3. support them from one moment to the next.
  4. grant unto them their lives. (V. 23.)
- C. So even if they should:
  1. render all the thanks and praise their souls possess (v. 20) and
  2. serve him with their whole souls (v. 21),
- D. they would still be unprofitable servants.
- E. But all he requires in return is to keep his commandments. (V. 22.)
- F. If they do, he immediately blesses them. (V. 24.)

G. Conclusions.
  1. Two reasons for our indebtedness to God:
     a. he created us and grants us life. (V. 23.)
     b. when we keep his commandments, he blesses us more, which only increases our indebtedness. (V. 24.)
  2. Man has nothing about which he can boast.
  3. Man is not even so much as the dust of the earth. (V. 25.)

Our Gratitude for Creation

King Benjamin initially stressed one aspect of God's graciousness, that God is responsible for our creation. By this, Benjamin seemed to have meant not just the making of our own bodies, but the whole of creation—the heavens, the earth, and all that in them are. That simple fact alone should be basis enough for our unending gratitude. When a man creates something through his own labor—a work of art, a building, a piece of furniture, great music—we say that it is his. In other words, we recognize that he has claim upon it, that he has stewardship over it, that he has the right to do with it as he wishes.

By that same principle, we should acknowledge that, because all that we see and know comes from the labor of God's hands, it is his. Therefore, whatever we have, or take, or use, or enjoy puts us automatically in his debt. In a revelation to the Prophet Joseph Smith, the Lord clearly stated that this is indeed the case: "For it is expedient that I, the Lord, should make every man accountable, as a steward over earthly blessings, *which I have made* and prepared for my creatures. I, the Lord, stretched out the heavens, and built the earth, *my very handiwork;* and *all things therein are mine.*" (D&C 104:13–14; italics added.) Note the possessive phrases used in those verses: "which I have made," "my very handiwork," "all things therein are mine." As the Psalmist said, "The earth is the Lord's, and the fulness thereof; the world, and they that dwell therein." (Ps. 24:1.)

Think for a moment how that simple concept would alter people's thinking if they would really accept it. We clutch things to our bosom and say, "These are mine." Individuals rob, cheat, and steal, or they manipulate and maneuver so they may be able to claim things as their own. Figuratively, the rich sit on their velvet thrones, drinking from golden goblets, and ignore the desperate sufferings of the poor because they think that what they have received belongs solely to them. Nations go to war over lands that they did nothing to create.

If we truly believed that God was the owner of all things, that man was only a user and a borrower, our approach to life would alter drastically. A classic illustration of that principle was the man Job. After facing devastating losses of family, property, and health, he stated simply: "Naked came I out of my mother's womb, and naked shall I return thither: the Lord gave, and the Lord hath taken away; blessed be the name of the Lord." (Job 1:21.) Henry B. Eyring spoke of this natural human tendency to forget all that God has done for us: "We so easily forget that we came into life with nothing. Whatever we get soon seems our natural right, not a gift. And we forget the giver. Then our gaze shifts from what we have been given to what we don't have yet. . . . The remembrance urged upon us by King Benjamin can be ours. *Remembrance is the seed of gratitude.*"[1]

Because some miracles are so commonly seen, we accept them as commonplace—an infant's birth, the coming of spring, the glory of a forested mountain range, the silent and undirected healing process within the human body, the never-ending procession of glorious sunrises and sunsets, the infinite variety and minute beauty of something so simple as snowflakes showering upon the earth in countless billions.

Those who try to duplicate nature in the laboratory still feel awestruck when they compare their own marvelous inventions with those of nature itself. In a *National Geographic* article on the recent development of new high-tech materials, Thomas Canby discussed such mind-boggling advances as ceramic ball bearings so tough that they leave dimples on an anvil when hammered by a blacksmith, but they do not break; a metal that actually hardens as its temperature rises; cement sheets thin and light enough that they are used in hang-glider fabric; plastics so flexible that they can be stretched as much as a thousand percent and grow stronger in the process! After quoting a scientist who said that his goal was to develop materials that respond as nature does, the author concludes: "[Their goal is to be] like nature. For materials scientists, the perfection of a tree, a bone, a spiderweb remain a distant goal."[2]

Numerous passages in scripture clearly state our obligations of feeling gratitude and giving thanks to God for all he has given. In language similar to that of the Ten Commandments (Thou shalt not steal, thou shalt honor thy parents, and so on), the Lord says: "Thou shalt thank the Lord thy God in all things." (D&C 59:7.) A few verses later, he said, "In nothing doth man offend God, or against none is his wrath kindled, save those who confess not his hand in all things, and obey not his commandments." (D&C 59:21.)

In March of 1832, the Lord tied thankfulness to both spiritual and temporal results when he said: "He who receiveth all things with thankfulness shall be made glorious; and the things of this earth shall be added unto him, even an hundred fold, yea, more." (D&C 78:19.) When we consider the richness of creation, God's inestimable abundance given freely to man, his power that sustains life, and the continual outpouring of those blessings when we are obedient, we ought to have no difficulty understanding why King Benjamin chose the word *indebtedness* to describe our state.

Unprofitable Servants

Now we come to two statements in King Benjamin's address that many Latter-day Saints may find a little troublesome. Unlike Calvinism and some other Christian sects, we do not look upon man as inherently evil. A crucial concept in our theology is that we are literally children of our Heavenly Father. "I am a child of God," we sing, "and he has sent me here."[3] We speak positively about the need for self-esteem and self-reliance. We speak of our potential to become Gods, a concept so daring as to cause many Christians to recoil at our boldness.

So how do we reconcile these ideas with King Benjamin's powerful "if" statements? He says that even *if* we should render all the praise and thanks our souls are capable of, and even *if* we should serve him with our whole souls, we would still be "unprofitable servants." (Mosiah 2:20–21.) Even more pointed (some might say more devastating) is his answer to his own rhetorical question: "Can ye say aught of yourselves?" Answer: "Ye cannot say that *ye are even as much* as the dust of the earth." (Mosiah 2:25; italics added.) Let's examine these two points one at a time, for they are pivotal in our understanding of the concept of divine indebtedness and the Atonement.

The Savior used the phrase "unprofitable servants" in a short parable he taught in response to the disciples' plea to him, "Increase our faith." (Luke 17:5.)

> Which of you, having a servant plowing or feeding cattle, will say unto him by and by, when he is come from the field, Go and sit down to meat? And will not rather say unto him, Make ready wherewith I may sup, and gird

> thyself, and serve me, till I have eaten and drunken; and afterward thou shalt eat and drink? Doth he thank that servant because he did the things that were commanded him? I trow not. So likewise ye, when ye shall have done all those things which are commanded you, say, We are unprofitable servants: we have done that which was our duty to do. (Luke 17:7–10.)

In some ways, this parable is no less troublesome than King Benjamin's statement. However, focusing on the word *profit* will help us better understand the concept of unprofitable servants. The word implies personal gain or benefit. *Profit* means an increase in assets or status or benefits.

That is the crux of the concept of man being an unprofitable servant. God is perfect—in knowledge, power, influence, and attributes. He is the Creator of *all* things! What could any person—or all people together for that matter—do to bring profit, (that is, an increase in assets, status, or benefits) to God?

A nineteenth-century scholar, commenting on this parable, stated that concept eloquently, when he noted that no man

> can work righteousness, in the smallest degree, beyond those powers which God has given them; and justice and equity require that they should exert those powers to the uttermost in the service of their Maker; and, after having acted thus, it may be justly said, *They have done only what it was their duty to do*. The nature of God is illimitable, and all the attributes of that nature are infinitely glorious: they cannot be *lessened* by the *transgressions* of his creatures, nor can they be *increased* by the uninterrupted, eternal *obedience,* and unceasing *hallelujahs,* of all the intelligent creatures that people the whole vortex of nature. When ages, beyond the power of arithmetic to sum up, have elapsed, it may be said of the most pure and perfect creatures, "ye are unprofitable servants." Ye have derived your being from the infinite fountain of life: ye are upheld by the continued

> energy of the Almighty: his glories are infinite and eternal, and your obedience and services, however excellent in themselves, and profitable to you, have added nothing, and can add nothing, to the absolute excellencies and glories of your God.[4]

That we are his children and he loves us is undeniable, and that situation puts us in a status far above any of his other creations. But we must somehow disabuse ourselves of any notion that we can bring personal profit to God by our actions. That would make God indebted to men, which is unthinkable. So this explains King Benjamin's ringing "ifs." Even *if* we were to serve him with all the power of our souls, even *if* we should render thanks with that same power (which very few, if any, of us ever do), we would still be unprofitable servants.

Less Than the Dust of the Earth

The comment that we are even less than the dust of the earth may, on the surface, seem a little more difficult to resolve. Has man no worth at all, as that would imply? An experience Moses had has an interesting parallel to King Benjamin's thinking here. Benjamin concluded that man is less than the dust of the earth immediately after he noted that God is the creator and sustainer of men. About a thousand years earlier, the prophet Moses was caught up in heavenly vision and was shown the creation of "the world . . . and all the children of men." (Moses 1:8.) Then the heavenly power withdrew, and Moses was left to himself. When he recovered a little from the experience, his first words were "Now, for this cause I know that man is nothing, which thing I never had supposed." (Moses 1:10.)

Something about the majesty and infinite awesomeness of the creation reminded both King Benjamin and Moses of man's puny and finite nature. Even when we sense our smallness, however, are we really *less than* the dust? The "less than" concept is what particularly stings. Nothingness is one thing, *worthlessness* quite another. On the surface, however, that is exactly what King Benjamin's phrase "ye cannot say that ye are even as much as the dust of the earth" (Mosiah 2:25) seems to imply. Let us examine the phrase and its uses in the scriptures for clues that may aid our understanding.

To begin with, "dust of the earth" is a scriptural phrase implying far more than mere dirt particles. We are told that man was created from the dust of the earth. (See Gen. 2:7.) Perhaps another word that would come close to what is implied by dust would be "the *elements* of the earth." In Latter-day Saint theology, we certainly do not believe that God pulled together a pile of mud, formed it into the shape of a man, and breathed life into it. A more accurate statement would be to say that God created the human body from the elements of the earth. Benjamin said then, to paraphrase, that we are not even as much as those elements.

Interestingly, Mormon is the one who gives us the clues to help us better understand King Benjamin's statement. Benjamin's words, as well as the angel's message that the king delivered to his people,[5] had such a powerful impact upon the people that they fell to the ground. Mormon commented significantly, "They had viewed themselves in their own *carnal state,* even less than the dust of the earth." (Mosiah 4:2; italics added.) What a significant clue! The carnal or natural man is what is less than the dust of the earth. King Benjamin apparently agreed. One of the first things he stated as he continued his address after his people had fallen to the ground was that his people had been awakened to a sense of "[their] nothingness, and [their] worthless and fallen state." (Mosiah 4:5.) Here again man's worthlessness is mentioned in the context of his fallen state.

Note that King Benjamin said that lack of humility (or

not remembering our own nothingness) leads us to a state he called "the natural man," a state he also described as being "an enemy to God." (Mosiah 2:37; 3:19.) In a similar vein, President Ezra Taft Benson specifically defined pride as enmity against God. "The central feature of pride is enmity—enmity toward God and enmity toward our fellowmen. Enmity means 'hatred toward, hostility to, or a state of opposition.' It is the power by which Satan wishes to reign over us. Pride is essentially competitive in nature. We pit our will against God's."[6]

This leads us to Mormon's later specific explanation of why man is less than the dust of the earth:

> How quick [are men] to be lifted up in pride; yea, how quick to boast, and do all manner of that which is iniquity; and how slow are they to remember the Lord their God, and to give ear unto his counsels, yea, how slow to walk in wisdom's paths! Behold, they do not desire that the Lord their God, who hath created them, should rule and reign over them; notwithstanding his great goodness and his mercy towards them, they do set at naught his counsels, and they will not that he should be their guide.
>
> O how great is the nothingness of the children of men; yea, even they are less than the dust of the earth. For behold, the dust of the earth moveth hither and thither, to the dividing asunder, at the command of our great and everlasting God. (Hel. 12:5–8.)

There is the key. Benjamin said that all God asks of us as payment on our indebtedness to him is that we obey his commandments. But the natural man or fallen man is disobedient. Even the elements of the earth respond to God's voice, but fallen man does not. He proceeds on his own sinful way, ignoring God's goodness to him and the indebtedness we owe to him. Therefore, man is even less than the dust of the earth.

King Benjamin made a second point in almost the same

breath as his "less than" statement: "But behold, it belongeth to him who created you." (Mosiah 2:25.) This is a profound chain of reason: (1) God created all things including the dust (or elements) of the earth, (2) man is made of those elements, and (3) therefore even man's body belongs to God. This again is a reflection on our willful nature: the dust of the earth obeys God's voice, but we, who are God's as much as the dust is, do not listen or follow.

Indebtedness and Atonement (Mosiah 2:26–3:27)

Benjamin inextricably linked our indebtedness and the Atonement. By emphasizing the concept of man's nothingness, he made the two concepts dependent on one another. If that interdependency were outlined according to Benjamin's teachings, it would look something like this:

I. MAN BY HIMSELF IS NOTHING. (2:19–25.)
   - A. Therefore, we are indebted to God. (Vv. 19–21, 23–24.)
   - B. As payment, all that is required is obedience. (Vv. 22, 24.)

II. A WARNING AGAINST DISOBEDIENCE. (2:26–41.)
   - A. King Benjamin discharged his obligation to warn the people. (Vv. 26–30.)
   - B. He gave a charge to keep the commandments under the new king. (V. 31.)
   - C. All must take care that they don't obey evil spirits. (Vv. 32–35.)
     1. He who does and dieth in his sins is damned. (V. 33.)
     2. This is a just wage for transgressing knowingly.
     3. All have been taught by prophets and scriptures (yet another reason for our indebtedness to God). (Vv. 34–35.)

D. If you knowingly transgress:
   1. you withdraw from the Spirit. (V. 36.)
   2. you receive no guidance on life's path.
   3. you become an enemy to God. (V. 37.)
   4. the Lord has no place in you.
   5. and don't repent, you will experience guilt, shame, pain, and torment. (Vv. 38–39.)

E. King Benjamin called on all to consider the two choices:
   1. the awful situation of transgressors. (V. 40.)
   2. the blessed state (temporal and spiritual) of the obedient. (V. 41.)

III. THE MESSAGE OF THE ANGEL. (3:1–27.)

A. Glad tidings of great joy. (Vv. 1–11.)
   1. God to come to earth and minister to men. (Vv. 5–8.)
   2. He will be crucified and resurrected. (Vv. 9–10.)
   3. He atones for those who ignorantly sin. (V. 11.)

B. Wo to the rebellious (those who transgress knowingly). (Vv. 12–13.)

C. The Law of Moses and the Atonement. (Vv. 14–15.)
   1. Law of Moses given because of the hardness of Israel's hearts. (V. 14.)
   2. The Mosaic law pointed to Christ. (V. 15.)
   3. But without the Atonement, it had no power to save.

D. The Atonement. (Vv. 16–23.)
   1. Little children are atoned for. (V. 16.)
   2. No other means but through Christ. (V. 17.)
   3. Men damned unless they become as children and believe in Christ. (V. 18.)
   4. The natural man is an enemy to God and will be unless he (v. 19):
      a. yields to the enticings of the Holy Spirit.
      b. puts off the natural man.
      c. becomes a saint through the Atonement.
      d. becomes as a child.

E. When knowledge of the Atonement spreads, none will be blameless but children. (Vv. 20–21.)
F. Those who reject his words are damned, and their punishments just. (Vv. 23–27.)

With this outline we clearly see that, once Benjamin established the concept of divine indebtedness, he moved immediately to the ultimate proof of our ingratitude—our disobedience—and the consequences of it. From there, he turned naturally to the only cure for those consequences, namely, the Atonement. In fact, the previous concepts establish a natural foundation for the concept of grace, though Benjamin never uses the word itself. The definition of grace as found in the LDS Bible Dictionary states that it is the "divine means of help or strength given through the bounteous mercy and love of Jesus Christ. . . . This grace is an enabling power that allows men and women to lay hold on eternal life and exaltation *after they have expended their own best efforts.*"[7]

Note that last phrase. It is another way of saying exactly what King Benjamin was saying, namely that, even if we thank him with all our souls, even if we serve him our whole lives (another way to describe "best efforts"), we would still be unprofitable servants. Because of this awful state we are in, there must be a higher source of help, some "enabling power" that takes us in our utter helplessness and lifts us to the point where we can overcome our carnal and fallen natures and become the sons and daughters of God.

After establishing our indebtedness to God, King Benjamin then joyfully reported the glad tidings of great joy (the word *gospel* means good news or glad tidings) that the angel had given him and asked him to share with his people. In the visitation, as Benjamin related, the angel had shown him the Savior's ministry. A discourse on the inability of the Law of Moses to save (outside of the Atonement) immediately followed, and then the angel turned directly to the Atonement and its saving power. Without Christ and his saving power, individuals are damned; they are destined to remain in their fallen state as natural and carnal, as enemies to God. But through the grace, or enabling power, of Jesus Christ, they can put off the natural man and become saints, sanctified and holy, thus able to return to God's presence.

Indebtedness and atonement—the two are interwoven in King Benjamin's thinking. The Atonement is both another reason for our indebtedness and the means by which we escape from being servants of sin. According to Benjamin, there are four things that create our indebtedness:

1. He created us and all that we have. (2:20–21.)
2. He preserves us from moment to moment. (2:21.)
3. All he asks in return is that we keep his commandments, which if we do, he immediately blesses us, only adding to our indebtedness. (2:22–24.)
4. He has sent the Savior and provided us a way to overcome our sins and be saved. (3:17–19.)

Obtaining and Retaining a Remission of Sins (Mosiah 4:1–30)

The two concepts of indebtedness and atonement, as delivered by King Benjamin, had a tremendous impact on the people. They cried for mercy and asked that the atoning blood of Christ be applied in their behalf so their sins could be forgiven. (Mosiah 4:2.) The Lord granted their request, and Mormon wrote that they received a remission of their sins. (V. 3.)

King Benjamin, filled with joy at what had happened, returned to the exact same theme with which he began. He talked about how the people could retain the remission of sins they had just experienced. Here, as in the first part of his address, the concept of indebtedness still heavily flavored his thinking. In fact, his opening thought summarized the context of his previous words. Note his chain of reasoning:

A. The knowledge of God has awakened you to a sense of your nothingness and your fallen state. (V. 5.)

B. A knowledge of God's goodness and of the Atonement leads to trust in God, diligence in keeping the commandments, and continuing in faith to the end. (V. 6.)

C. These are what lead to salvation. (V. 7.)

D. There is no other way. (V. 8.)

E. We retain a remission of sins by remembering God's goodness and our own nothingness and unworthiness. (V. 11.)

F. This remembrance will influence all we do and lead us to eternal life. (Vv. 12–30.)

Thus the key to the whole process of salvation is remembering, and the primary focus of our remembrance is (1) God's goodness and greatness, (2) our own nothingness, and (3) God's greatest gift, that of his own Son to make us whole. President Ezra Taft Benson said:

> The Prophet Joseph said at one time that one of the greatest sins of which the Latter-day Saints would be guilty of is the sin of ingratitude. I presume most of us have not thought of that as a great sin. There is a great tendency for us in our prayers and in our pleadings with the Lord to ask for additional blessings. But sometimes I feel we need to devote more of our prayers to expressions of gratitude and thanksgiving for blessing already received. We enjoy so much. Of course we need daily blessings of the Lord, but if we sin in the matter of prayer, I think it is in the lack of our expressions of thanksgiving, for blessings that we receive daily.[8]

How simple a thing, this matter of gratitude. Perhaps that is why so many so easily overlook it. But in the matchless address of this humble, righteous monarch, we are taught the profound consequences that can result from gratitude or lack of it. Benjamin did not seek to invoke a sense of hopelessness when he noted that we are less than the dust of the earth. He sought instead to instill a sense of humility and, more especially, a sense of our utter and total dependence upon God for all that we have, all that we are, and all that we can be.

Chapter 11

"Faith in the Lord Jesus Christ"

(Article of Faith 4)

Even without the fourth Article of Faith, which lists "faith in the Lord Jesus Christ" as the first principle of the gospel, it would be obvious to anyone opening the Standard Works that faith is a pervasive, all-encompassing principle. The word itself and its cognate forms are found hundreds of times. Its importance in the plan of salvation could best be summarized by Paul's statement that "without faith it is impossible to please him: for he that cometh to God must believe that he is, and that he is a rewarder of them that diligently seek him." (Heb. 11:6.) Joseph Smith, commenting on that verse, said, "If it should be asked—Why is it impossible to please God without faith? The answer would be—Because without faith it is impossible for men to be saved; and as God desires the salvation of men, he must, of course, desire that they should have faith; and he could not be pleased unless they had, or else he could be pleased with their destruction."[1]

Clearly, then, faith is at the center of all that we do and teach in the gospel of Jesus Christ. Unfortunately, however, in the Church we occasionally find some whose attitude seems to be that, since it is the first principle of the gospel, it is also a simple principle, easily comprehended and left behind as one moves on to more complicated and challenging areas of study. However, this is not the case. Elder Vaughn J. Featherstone has summed up, as well as any, the challenge of studying faith as a concept:

> What a great thing it is if we understand what faith is. What is faith? How does it work? Do you have total faith? When we come to a full and total understanding of faith, then I think we ought to move on to repentance. When we understand that totally, then we should move through the principles. But I doubt we will ever really get through an understanding and complete knowledge of faith in a lifetime. I don't care how intellectual you are, or how long you study, I doubt you will ever come to an end of the study of faith, the first principle of the gospel. The gospel is so simple that a fool will not err therein, but it is so beautiful and so sophisticated that I believe the greatest intellectual can make a study of faith and never come to an end of understanding.[2]

Faith—a Principle of Power

If a typical Church group were to give a one-word synonym for faith, the usual answers would be *belief, trust, assurance, hope,* and so on. Joseph Smith's *Lectures on Faith* gives a different definition for faith, one that has profound implication for our understanding. In the first lecture, commenting on Hebrews 11:3, the Prophet said:

> Faith is not only the principle of action, but of power also, in all intelligent beings, whether in heaven or on earth. Thus says the author of the epistle to the Hebrews (11:3):
>
> "Through faith we understand that the worlds were framed by the word of God; so that things which are seen were not made of things which do appear."
>
> By this we understand that the principle of power which existed in the bosom of God, by which the worlds were framed, was faith; and that it is by reason of this principle

> of power existing in the Deity, that all created things exist; so that all things in heaven, on earth, or under the earth exist by reason of faith as it existed in HIM.
>
> Had it not been for the principle of faith the worlds would never have been framed, neither would man have been formed of the dust. It is the principle by which Jehovah works, and through which he exercises power over all temporal as well as eternal things. Take this principle or attribute—for it is an attribute—from the Deity, and he would cease to exist.
>
> Who cannot see, that if God framed the worlds by faith, that it is by faith that he exercises power over them, and that faith is the principle of power? And if the principle of power, it must be so in man as well as in the Deity? This is the testimony of all the sacred writers, and the lesson which they have been endeavoring to teach to man.[3]

That faith is a principle of power is evident in scripture. As we look in the Standard Works and find examples of men with faith, we find in virtually every case demonstrations of tremendous and marvelous power. We read about Enoch, for example, speaking the word of the Lord, and the earth trembling and the mountains fleeing! (See Moses 7:13.) We see Joshua saying, "Sun, stand thou still"; and the sun obeys! (See Josh. 10:12–14.) Or we find Peter spying a lame man near a gate of the temple—a man with a congenital birth defect who had been unable to walk for the forty years of his life. Peter said, simply, "In the name of Jesus Christ of Nazareth rise up and walk." The record states, "And he leaping up stood, and walked, and entered with them into the temple, walking, and leaping, and praising God." (Acts 3:1–10.) Faith is the power by which God speaks, creating worlds, solar systems, and universes. So when we speak of faith, we speak of tremendous power, not only physical power, but even power that can save a man from temporal and spiritual death.

Requirements for Developing Faith

In the third lecture on faith, Joseph Smith described what is necessary for people to have faith sufficient to bring them salvation:

> Let us here observe, that three things are necessary in order that any rational and intelligent being may exercise faith in God unto life and salvation.
>
> First, the idea that he actually exists.
>
> Secondly, a *correct* idea of his character, perfections, and attributes.
>
> Thirdly, an actual knowledge that the course of life which he is pursuing is according to his will. For without an acquaintance with these three important facts, the faith of every rational being must be imperfect and unproductive; but with this understanding it can become perfect and fruitful, abounding in righteousness, unto the praise and glory of God the Father, and the Lord Jesus Christ.[4]

Looking at these three requirements carefully, we can see that each of the three involves knowledge; that is, we have *an idea* in the first one, *a correct idea* in the second one, and an *actual knowledge* in the third one. If a sequence were designed depicting an individual's movement toward salvation, it would look something like this:

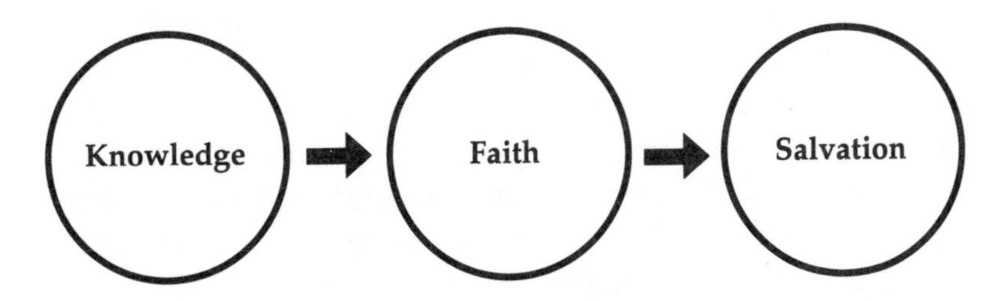

In other words, if we are to achieve salvation, we must have faith; and if we are to have faith, we must have knowledge. This is a crucial thing to know about faith and the means to develop it, and yet it raises a troubling question. If we say that knowledge is the requirement or prerequisite of faith, someone will invariably ask, But if knowledge leads to faith, how do you explain Alma 32, wherein Alma describes the process of faith leading to salvation as having faith first, which *then* leads us to a perfect knowledge?

After carefully rereading Alma 32 and studying the *Lectures on Faith,* I have come to some tentative conclusions about faith. Suppose, for instance, that faith in Jesus Christ is a *process* rather than simply a concept? Suppose that the same word is used by different prophets to describe different phases or stages of the process? Could that explain what seems to be a different use of the same term? And if that is true, can the process be described? Do the scriptures describe it? I believe that they do and that the best descriptions of that process are found within the Book of Mormon itself. In an attempt to describe this process, I have developed a paradigm, or model, of what the process of faith in Jesus Christ is.

Some words of caution need to be given, however, before we begin looking at the model itself. First, one danger of any model is that it tends to oversimplify. This is of value in one way, because the simplification helps us to conceptualize or grasp the relationships of a complex subject. But when we begin to apply the model closely to reality, we find that it may not hold up in all cases. Exceptions will exist that do not truly fit the model. The paradigm of faith included in this chapter is only to help people conceptualize a grand and complex subject. Second, Elder Featherstone's comment that the study of faith can be pursued without ever reaching the end of understanding suggests that the model presented here should be refined or adapted as an individual pursues a deeper understanding of faith. Third, the model is based heavily on three major sections in the Book of Mormon dealing with faith in Jesus Christ: Alma 32, Ether 12, and Moroni 7. Thus understanding the paradigm is based in part upon a thorough study of those chapters.

The Process We Call Faith

One of the challenges in describing or discussing faith is the idea that faith is a process involving various stages of development. A prophet may use the word *faith* to speak of faith as a whole or to refer to any one of the different stages of the process. This presents a challenge in studying the scriptures, and sometimes even results in confusion. Joseph Smith, for example, said that faith is power; Alma said that faith is hope. Both, however, can be easily understood if we use the process model of faith.

The tendency for prophets to use one word—*faith*—to discuss different aspects of faith makes it difficult to delineate the different stages of the process. After some consideration, I decided that, rather than try to generate new terms—terms the prophets did not use—I would instead use the basic word with a number subscript, thus describing the stages of the process as $faith_1$, $faith_2$, and so on. In addition, it seems to me that each stage of faith always contains three basic components: hope, action, and confirmation. Again, because these may differ somewhat in their nature, depending on which level of the process of faith a person is at, I have chosen to designate these with subscripts too: $hope_1$, $hope_2$; $action_1$, $action_2$; $confirmation_1$, $confirmation_2$; and so on.

To begin, let us examine Alma 32. I have concluded after studying the chapter that it describes the initial process of the development of faith in Jesus Christ, or, in terms of our nomenclature, the development of $faith_1$. Remember that Alma was speaking to the Zoramites, or, more precisely, a group of Zoramites who had been expelled from the congregations of the Zoramite churches because of their poor, lower-class status. The Zoramites had apostatized from the Nephites – they worshiped idols and had developed a proud and perverted way of worshiping. (See Alma 31:8–23, 31.) In other words, Alma was not speaking to members of Christ's church in the sermon recorded in Alma 32. Rather, he was speaking to a group who had just begun the process of developing faith. This situation has some important implications for Alma's discussion of faith.

When Alma spoke to these Zoramite poor, he seemed to have used the terms *faith* and *perfect knowledge* in a peculiar sense; that is, in a sense different from the normal usage of the terms. He equated faith with a hope or desire to believe what is not known to be true. Notice what he said in verse twenty-one of Alma 32: "Now as I said concerning faith – faith is not to have a perfect knowledge of things; therefore if ye have faith ye hope for things which are not seen, which are true." Notice that he said, "If ye have faith ye hope." In other words, he seemed to be defining faith as a hope or desire that the things he was telling them were true. He also limited his definition of faith to hoping for things that are actually true. That suggests that hoping for things that are untrue will not bring the results he described in the rest of the sermon.

Alma's use of the term *perfect knowledge* is revealed in verses eighteen to thirty-four. In verse eighteen he said, "If a man knoweth a thing he hath no cause to believe, for he knoweth it." In verse thirty-three, after telling the Zoramites how to experiment with the word, which he compared to a seed, he said that, when they begin to see it "swell" and "grow" in them, they must *know* that the seed is good. In other words, they didn't have to *hope* or desire to believe that it is good; they would know that it was good. Therefore he said in verse thirty-four, "Your knowledge is perfect in that thing." Obviously, he was not talking about perfect knowledge in any grand or universal sense; and he made that clear in verses thirty-five and thirty-six by saying that, once they had tasted this light, their knowledge was not perfect in an ultimate sense.

Notice also in Alma 32 that Alma gave two prerequisites for the development of faith (the very first level of faith). These prerequisites are, first, humility (see v. 16) and, second, hearing the word (see v. 23). If we are not willing to humble ourselves and make the experiment, we can never develop faith. Even more fundamental, if we do not have the word of the Lord on which to experiment, if we do not have knowledge or information on which to begin to believe, we cannot have faith. (For additional references, see also Moro. 7:24–25; Rom. 10:13–17.)

Level One: Faith or Hope

At each stage of faith, we must move through three components to reach the next level. Note the diagram of the first level of faith, or faith_1 on the following page. The three components are shown in their proper relationship to one another.

Hope_1, or the initial level of hope, would be the beginning step for the whole process. This level of hope is really nothing more than the desire or wish that something be true. It is as though we are motivated to say, "I want to know if this is true." Notice in verse twenty-seven, Alma said, "Even if ye can no more than *desire* to believe." (Italics added.) If we have hope_1, then we will be motivated to action_1, which is the second step of the process, or the second component of faith. At the first level of faith, this action may be no more than a willingness to try to ascertain whether the word we have heard is true.

Moroni taught a valuable concept about this level of faith when he wrote, "I would show unto the world that faith is

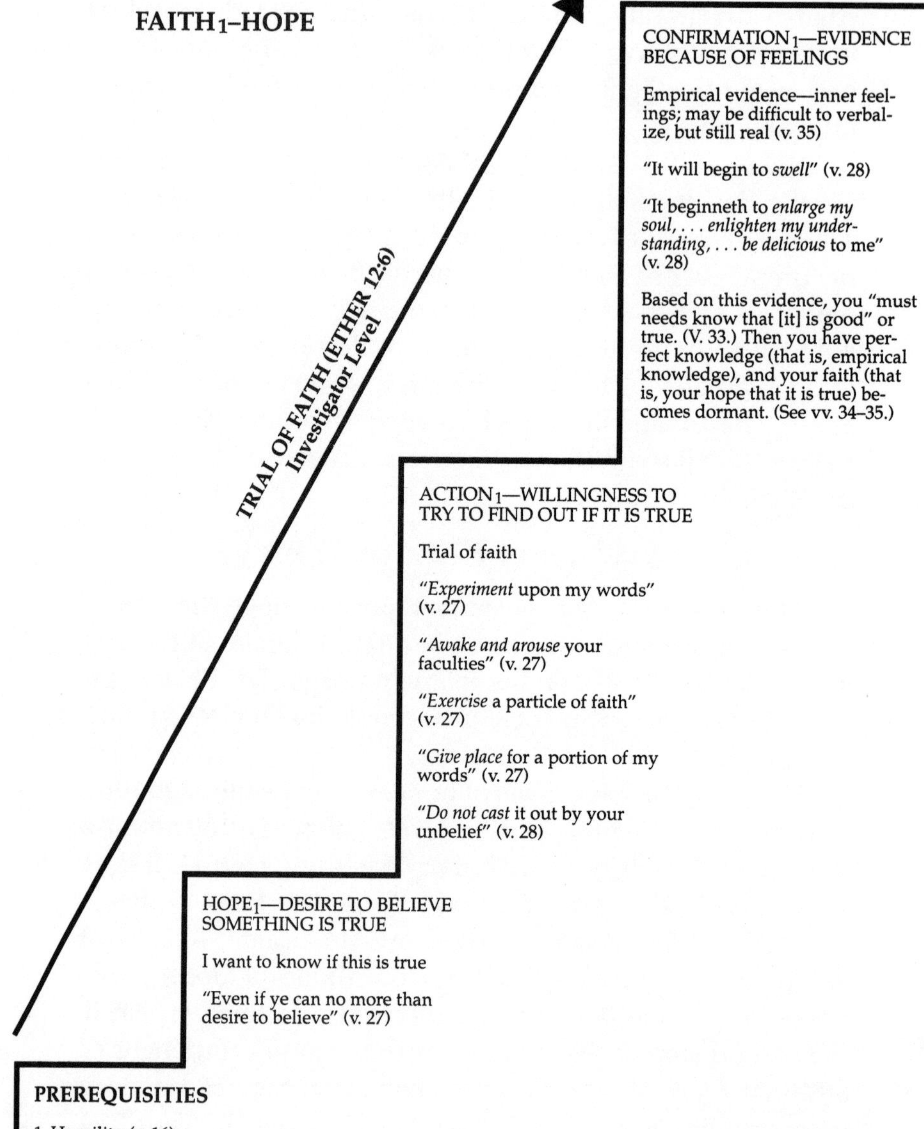

PREREQUISITIES

1. Humility (v. 16)
2. Hearing the word (v. 23)

(See also Moro. 7:24–25; Rom. 10:13-17.)

Note: Unless otherwise indicated, references in this chart are in Alma 32. Italics have been added.

things which are hoped for and not seen." (Ether 12:6.) This is essentially what Paul told us in Hebrews 11:1. In this case, faith, or the ability to trust in something not seen, is quite clear. We cannot "see" that the word we have heard is true; that is, we do not have empirical proof (proof based upon observation or experience) of the truthfulness of the word. Therefore, we must act on faith: we must trust or hope for something to be, although it is not yet based on seen evidence.

Moroni continued the verse by writing, "Dispute not because ye see not, for ye receive no witness until after the trial of your faith." In every case, in every level of the development of faith, there must be a trial of faith. That is, we are tested to see whether we will act on the basis of the hope that is in us. We have to show that we are motivated to behave according to the truths the Lord has given us, before we have actual evidence that these things are true. Notice again what Alma told the Zoramite poor in Alma 32:27–28, "If ye will awake and arouse your faculties, even to an experiment upon my words, and exercise a particle of faith, yea, even if ye can no more than desire to believe, let this desire work in you, even until ye believe in a manner that ye can give place for a portion of my words. . . . If ye do not cast it [the word] out by your unbelief, . . . it will begin to swell within your breasts." Notice the verbs of action that he used: *awake, arouse, exercise, desire, give place, not cast out*. We must act on our desire ($hope_1$) to know if the word of the Lord is true. This initial level of action ($action_1$) is basically one of will, one of deciding to try to find out if the word is true.

When we act by experimenting, awaking, exercising, and so on, we are led to the third component of faith, which is a confirmation of our hope. This initial level of the faith process would be called $confirmation_1$. Alma described this kind of evidence through feelings. Though this evidence is available only to the senses, it is still empirical, or real, evidence. It may be difficult to put into words, but that doesn't lessen its reality. Notice how Alma described this evidence through one's feelings, "It will begin to swell within your breasts; . . . it beginneth to enlarge [the] soul; yea, it beginneth to enlighten [the] understanding, yea, it beginneth to be delicious." (V. 28.)

Based on this real, though difficult-to-express evidence, we can say, as Alma did in verse thirty-three, "Ye must needs *know* that the seed is good." (Italics added.) In other words, we now have knowledge based on empirical evidence. Alma called this "perfect knowledge." That perfect knowledge gained through the trial of faith and confirmed by real evidence then does away with the faith described by Alma (to the nonfaithful Zoramites), the faith that is a hope or desire to believe what is not known to be true. Since we have come to *know* that the word is good, we no longer need to *hope* that it is good. Perfect knowledge takes away or swallows up faith, as Alma used the term.

When we move through the trial of faith (hope that moves us to act, which leads to a confirmation of that hope), we can say that we have achieved the first stage of faith. These preliminary steps are at an investigator level: we are investigating whether something is true. Alma's description and discussion fit the Zoramite needs perfectly. Typically, we would hypothesize that when a person begins the process of developing and entering into $faith_1$, described so perfectly by Alma, he will likely get confirmation quite rapidly. This is an experience missionaries see countless times. When people truly humble themselves upon hearing the word of God and experiment upon that word (for instance, seeking to know through prayer whether something is true), very often the confirmation, the swelling, the feeling of truthfulness, the almost indescribable sensation that this is good come quickly, and they know that the word of the Lord is a good seed.

Level Two: Faith or Knowledge

When we have achieved $faith_1$, have we achieved all that there is to have? Obviously not. Alma himself encouraged the people to continue on once they had received this "perfect knowledge." He told them to nourish the seed that was starting to grow until it became a great tree providing them with the fruit of eternal life. (See verses 25–43.) In other words, once we have $faith_1$, we can move on to the next level of the process in developing faith. The second stage of faith ($faith_2$), diagrammed on the following page, is a level of faith entailing belief and knowledge.

Once again there are the three components: $hope_2$, $action_2$, and $confirmation_2$. In the second level of hope, we have more than a desire to know if something is true. Now our attitude could be described not as "I want to know if this is true," but as "I desire this truth." As Moroni stated it, we may "with surety hope for a better world." (Ether 12:4.) This is a major step upward from the $faith_1$ level. In his sermon to the Zoramites, Alma did not discuss in detail this second level of faith (probably because of the nature of his audience). But others did. Besides Moroni's statement in Ether 12:4 above, we find statements like these from Mormon: You "shall have hope through the atonement of Christ . . . to be raised unto life eternal" (Moro. 7:41); or, "Without faith [could this be $faith_1$?] there cannot be any hope" (Moro. 7:42).

When we move into this second level of hope ($hope_2$), where we begin to sincerely believe in the things we have heard rather than simply desiring to believe, we will then be motivated to action again. However, this action ($action_2$) is on a higher level than that of $faith_1$ and could be defined as a willingness to live the truths we believe to be true. Whereas

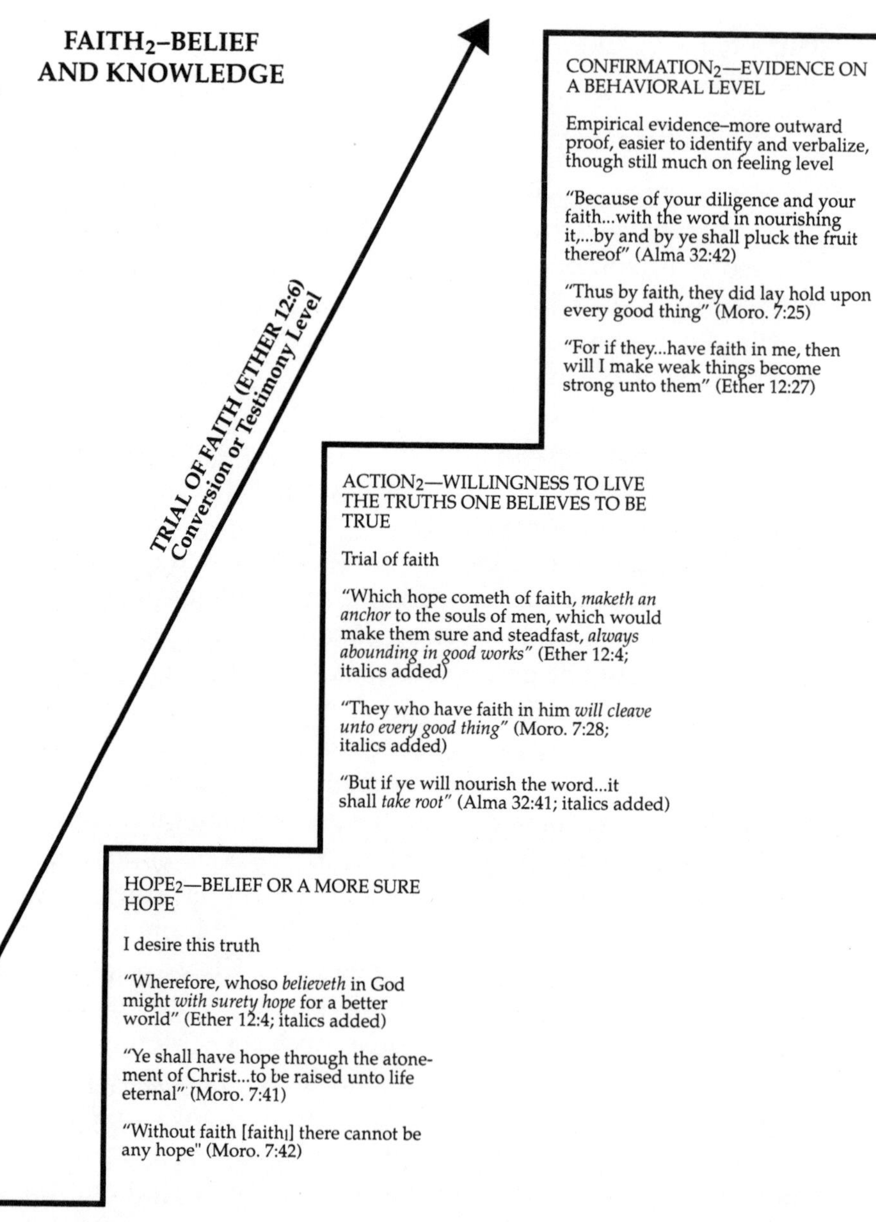
FAITH$_2$–BELIEF
AND KNOWLEDGE
TRIAL OF FAITH (ETHER 12:6)
Conversion or Testimony Level
CONFIRMATION$_2$—EVIDENCE ON A BEHAVIORAL LEVEL
Empirical evidence–more outward proof, easier to identify and verbalize, though still much on feeling level
"Because of your diligence and your faith...with the word in nourishing it,...by and by ye shall pluck the fruit thereof" (Alma 32:42)
"Thus by faith, they did lay hold upon every good thing" (Moro. 7:25)
"For if they...have faith in me, then will I make weak things become strong unto them" (Ether 12:27)
ACTION$_2$—WILLINGNESS TO LIVE THE TRUTHS ONE BELIEVES TO BE TRUE
Trial of faith
"Which hope cometh of faith, *maketh an anchor* to the souls of men, which would make them sure and steadfast, *always abounding in good works*" (Ether 12:4; italics added)
"They who have faith in him *will cleave unto every good thing*" (Moro. 7:28; italics added)
"But if ye will nourish the word...it shall *take root*" (Alma 32:41; italics added)
HOPE$_2$—BELIEF OR A MORE SURE HOPE
I desire this truth
"Wherefore, whoso *believeth* in God might *with surety hope* for a better world" (Ether 12:4; italics added)
"Ye shall have hope through the atonement of Christ...to be raised unto life eternal" (Moro. 7:41)
"Without faith [faith$_1$] there cannot be any hope" (Moro. 7:42)
CONFIRMATION$_1$

we had previously acted to find out if the Lord's word were true, now we act to incorporate into our lives the truths we have learned. Here again we find in operation the principle in Ether 12:6: we must have our faith tried; we must prove by our actions that the hope in us truly is sincere and serious. Notice what Moroni said about this hope: it makes "an anchor to the souls of men, which would make them sure and steadfast, always abounding in good works." (Ether 12:4.) In his letter on faith, hope, and charity, Mormon said, "They who have faith in him will cleave unto every good thing." (Moro. 7:28.) This seems to be what Alma meant when he said, "If ye nourish [the word] with much care it will get root." (Alma 32:37.)

When we operate at the $action_2$ level, we again undergo the trial of faith. We must show that we are willing to trust in things not seen. When we do so, we receive confirmation ($confirmation_2$), specifically evidence on a behavioral level. This empirical evidence is more outward than that received in $confirmation_1$, where the evidence consisted mostly of inner feelings (although $confirmation_2$ still includes many feelings). Such evidence is easier to identify and to put into words. It would involve statements such as "Yes, my prayer was answered"; or "I can see that this principle works in my life." Such confirmation leads us to say not "I believe," but "*I know* the gospel is true." The word has grown to the point where we can actually begin to taste the fruits of it in our lives. (See Alma 32:42.) In Moroni 7:25 we read, "Thus by faith, they did lay hold upon every good thing."

Now that we have examined the first two levels of faith, we begin to appreciate the profound implications of the discussion of faith and works James the apostle gave. If we do not have works joined to our faith, then our faith is dead, "being alone." (See James 2:17.) If we have the hope or desire that something is true ($hope_1$) but refuse to act on that hope, we will receive no confirmation, and our faith, even at this early stage, will be dead. The same is true in level two. Once we believe that something is true but refuse to live the truth, then we have faith without works, and our faith dies. We will receive no confirmation. The confirmation comes only after the trial of faith. But in this second level, our trial is not on an investigator level; we are tried on a higher level involving conversion, or testimony.

Level Three—Faith or Power

Now we are prepared to look at the next level of faith, which brings us to faith as Joseph Smith defined it. We could say that faith_3, diagrammed on the following page, is the power level of faith. Once again we are describing a major step upward from the previous level, and once again we find all three components operating as in the previous levels.

Hope_1 is to hope that something is true; and hope_2 is to believe that it is true. After having gone through the process of faith_2, however, we have confirmation and knowledge that the things we cannot see are indeed true. This makes a new level of hope possible. Hope_3, the third level of hope, could be described as a knowledge and assurance of things not seen. At this level, our attitude is reflected by this statement: I have the truth, and I desire to use it to become like God. This is, I believe, what Moroni meant by the phrase, "a more excellent hope." (Ether 12:32.) This desire seems to also describe what Nephi meant by "a perfect brightness of hope." (2 Ne. 31:20.) When our hope is this strong, when we truly have knowledge and assurance of unseen things, we move into more committed action (action_3). This higher level of action could be described as a willingness to do whatever God requires of a person. This, again, is a great trial of faith. Action_3 may involve a wide range of behaviors, including working on a Church welfare project or taking care of a sick

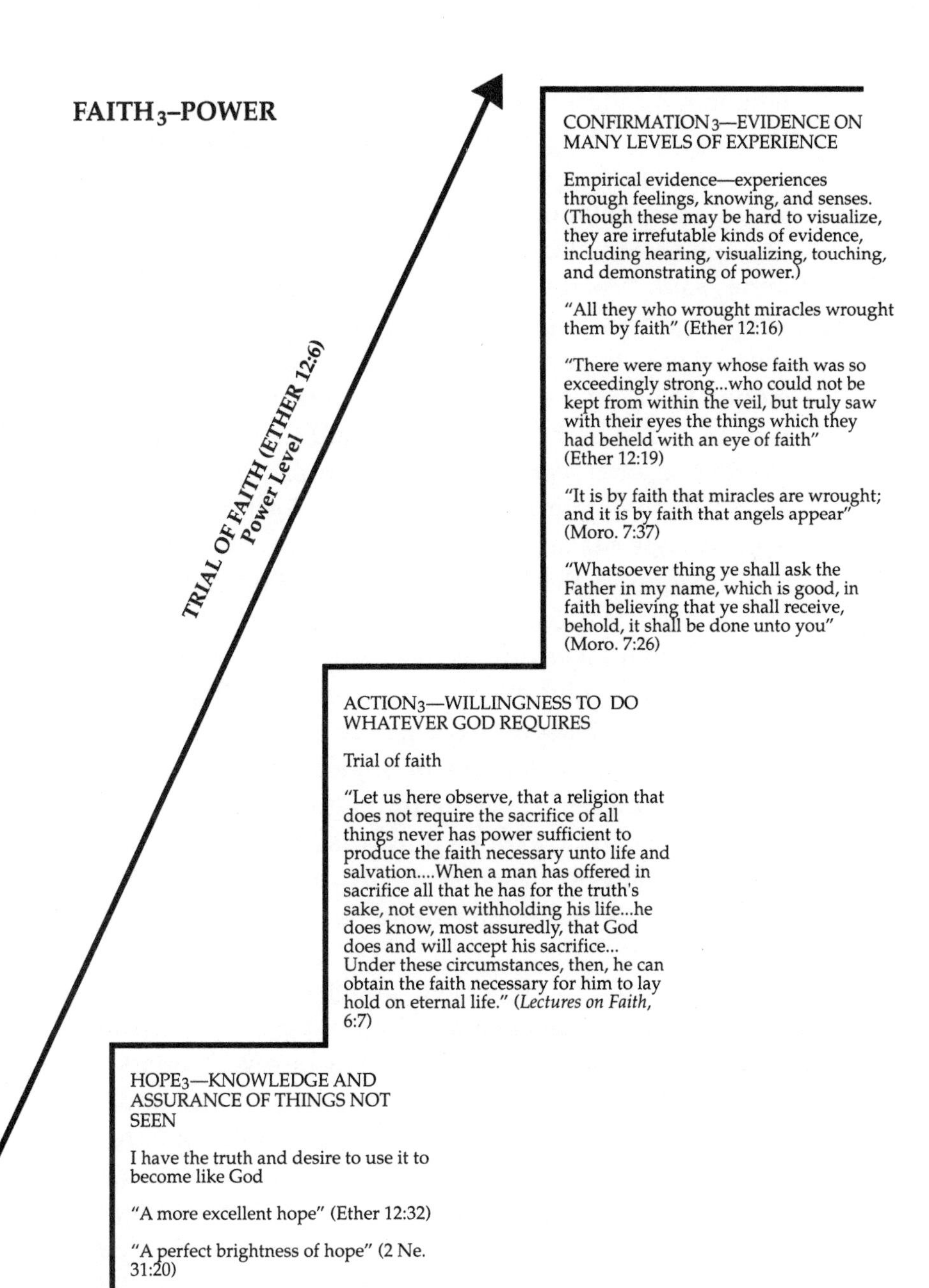
FAITH3–POWER
TRIAL OF FAITH (ETHER 12:6)
Power Level
CONFIRMATION3—EVIDENCE ON MANY LEVELS OF EXPERIENCE
Empirical evidence—experiences through feelings, knowing, and senses. (Though these may be hard to visualize, they are irrefutable kinds of evidence, including hearing, visualizing, touching, and demonstrating of power.)
"All they who wrought miracles wrought them by faith" (Ether 12:16)
"There were many whose faith was so exceedingly strong...who could not be kept from within the veil, but truly saw with their eyes the things which they had beheld with an eye of faith" (Ether 12:19)
"It is by faith that miracles are wrought; and it is by faith that angels appear" (Moro. 7:37)
"Whatsoever thing ye shall ask the Father in my name, which is good, in faith believing that ye shall receive, behold, it shall be done unto you" (Moro. 7:26)
ACTION3—WILLINGNESS TO DO WHATEVER GOD REQUIRES
Trial of faith
"Let us here observe, that a religion that does not require the sacrifice of all things never has power sufficient to produce the faith necessary unto life and salvation....When a man has offered in sacrifice all that he has for the truth's sake, not even withholding his life...he does know, most assuredly, that God does and will accept his sacrifice... Under these circumstances, then, he can obtain the faith necessary for him to lay hold on eternal life." (Lectures on Faith, 6:7)
HOPE3—KNOWLEDGE AND ASSURANCE OF THINGS NOT SEEN
I have the truth and desire to use it to become like God
"A more excellent hope" (Ether 12:32)
"A perfect brightness of hope" (2 Ne. 31:20)
CONFIRMATION2

neighbor's children. It may be something as trying and challenging as God's request to Abraham that he sacrifice his only son.

In our development of faith, if we have reached this point of hope or knowledge but refuse to act accordingly, then, as James said, "As the body without the spirit is dead, so faith without works is dead also." (James 2:26.) We have failed the trial of faith and will receive no confirmation of our hope. Notice the quotation by Joseph Smith from the *Lectures on Faith* included in the diagram. He said that only a willingness to sacrifice whatever God requires brings the knowledge that allows us to obtain the faith required for for salvation.[5]

If we operate at this level of action, we would expect that confirmation of this hope would be forthcoming, and such is the case. We could describe this level of confirmation (confirmation$_3$) as evidence on many levels of experience. It can not only involve experiences of inner feelings and knowledge, but also include experiences available to the senses, such as visions, visitations of angels, the demonstration of power in miracles, speaking in tongues, and the like. These may still be hard to express in words (in the sense that words are inadequate to describe them), but they are irrefutable kinds of evidence, demonstrations that the honest person cannot deny.

Notice the promises cited under the confirmation$_3$ level in the diagram. This is what the Lord meant when he said, "These signs shall follow them that believe." (Mark 16:17.) This power level of faith also helps us to better understand what the Lord meant when he said: "Faith cometh not by signs, but signs follow those that believe. Yea, signs come by faith, not by the will of men, nor as they please, but by the will of God. Yea, signs come by faith, unto mighty works, for without faith no man pleaseth God." (D&C 63:9–11.)

I believe that understanding the process of faith$_3$ also

gives us added insight as to why those who seek signs to bolster faith are called "a wicked and adulterous generation." (Matt. 16:4.) A person who wants to build his faith only on the basis of confirmation or evidence, without living the principles, seeks to circumvent the trial of faith that Moroni described. That is, he wants to have confirmation without paying the price of hope and action. And this "adulterates" or pollutes the proper relationship in the developmental process of faith. Satan seems to understand the significance of this and often prompts his servants to demand a sign, to demand faith without paying any price. (See, for example, Jacob 7:13; Alma 30:43; Ether 12:5.)

Level Four—Faith or Perfection

In level three of faith, or the power level, we looked to the faith shown by the people in the scriptures whom we typically characterize as having great faith. Many people might think of this as being the highest level of faith, but I feel that there is a fourth level of faith, which could be described as the perfection level.

Once again, this is a major step upward. We have to be a little more speculative as we describe this level of the process of faith because relatively few have achieved it; and those who have seem reticent (by direction of the Spirit) to talk about it in much detail. But I believe again that it involves our three components of hope, action, and confirmation, as diagrammed on the following page.

In level three, hope involved knowledge and assurance. How could one come to a higher level than that? I suggest that $hope_4$ is the actual knowledge that one will become like God, and it can be characterized by the attitude, I desire to be as God is. Two scriptures come to mind: "The more sure word of prophecy means a *man's knowing that he is sealed up* unto eternal life" (D&C 131:5, italics added); and, "If ye do

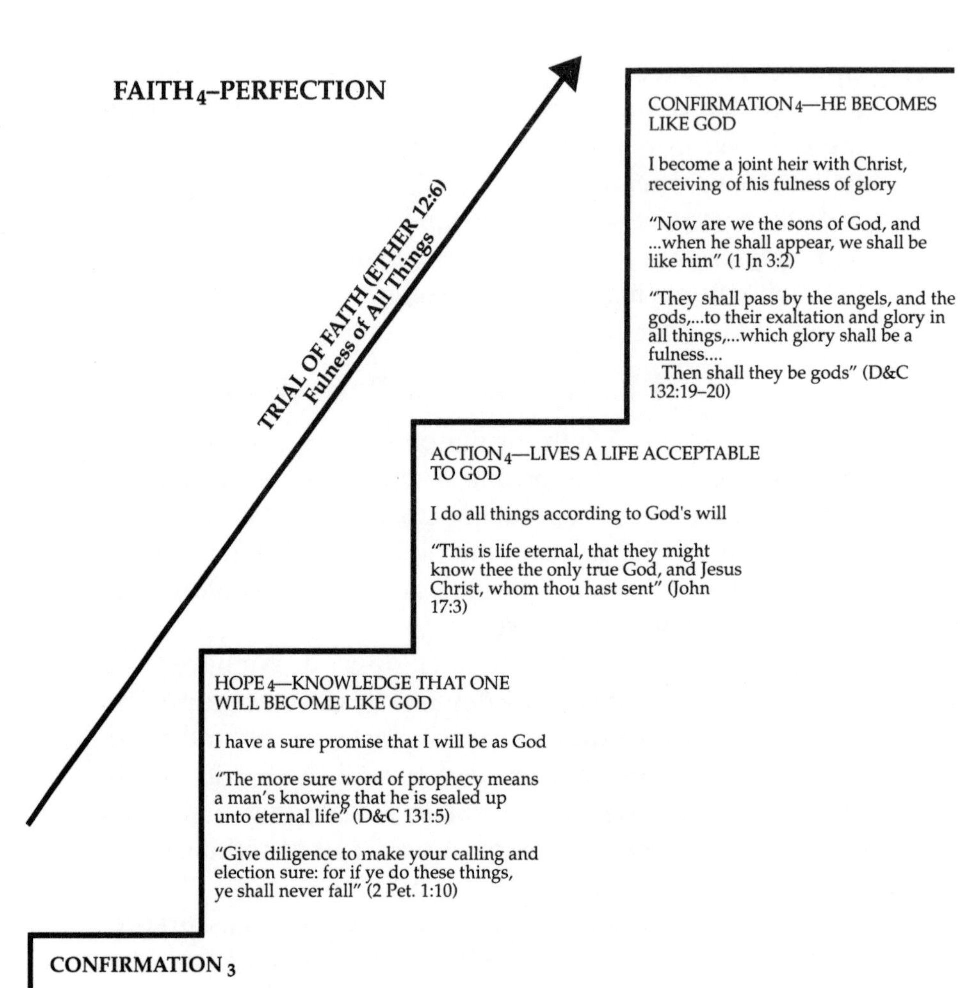

FAITH 4–PERFECTION
TRIAL OF FAITH (ETHER 12:6)
Fulness of All Things
CONFIRMATION 4—HE BECOMES LIKE GOD
I become a joint heir with Christ, receiving of his fulness of glory
"Now are we the sons of God, and ...when he shall appear, we shall be like him" (1 Jn 3:2)
"They shall pass by the angels, and the gods,...to their exaltation and glory in all things,...which glory shall be a fulness....
Then shall they be gods" (D&C 132:19–20)
ACTION 4—LIVES A LIFE ACCEPTABLE TO GOD
I do all things according to God's will
"This is life eternal, that they might know thee the only true God, and Jesus Christ, whom thou hast sent" (John 17:3)
HOPE 4—KNOWLEDGE THAT ONE WILL BECOME LIKE GOD
I have a sure promise that I will be as God
"The more sure word of prophecy means a man's knowing that he is sealed up unto eternal life" (D&C 131:5)
"Give diligence to make your calling and election sure: for if ye do these things, ye shall never fall" (2 Pet. 1:10)
CONFIRMATION 3

these things, *ye shall never fall*" (2 Pet. 1:10, italics added), which is Peter's promise to those who were laboring to make their calling and election sure.

When someone has reached this level of faith in mortality, his calling and election is made sure, and he is told by the more sure word of prophecy that he will be exalted. Imagine the level of hope or desire that such a revelation would create in him. Such hope would lead him to the fourth or highest level of action ($action_4$)—the level where his life becomes more and more godlike until he is made perfect and becomes worthy to become a god. Whether the phrase "trial of faith" adequately describes $action_4$ is not important. What is important is to know that the person must still live at a level of action commensurate with the level of hope within him. When he does so, he will receive a level of confirmation also commensurate with his level of action. In the highest level of confirmation ($confirmation_4$), a man receives the ultimate proof of the truths of the gospel—he is made a god!

As discussed at the beginning, the paradigm of the four levels of faith in Jesus Christ is inadequate to describe all the complexities of faith. Certainly it needs further clarification and refinement. But I have found it to be tremendously helpful as I think through what the prophets have said about faith. When Joseph Smith said faith is power, he was obviously speaking about a different level of faith than when Alma said to experiment upon his words so that faith could be swallowed up in perfect knowledge.

I also find it helpful to think of the three components—hope, action, and confirmation—at each level of faith, for I find the three principles operating in the lives of those who demonstrate faith. These principles also have relationship to repentance, baptism, and enduring to the end. Often we risk the danger of becoming sign seekers by talking of having one's calling and election made sure. As we talk about this important concept, we must clearly define the price to be paid so we do not end up testing God. Rather, we should operate according to the level of knowledge and hope that the Lord has granted us. Then we will receive a greater and greater confirmation until Jesus Christ makes us joint heirs with him, and we become gods. I firmly believe that this is the process that we must follow in our lives if we are to find that power. Joseph Smith said this:

> All the saints of whom we have account, in all the revelations of God which are extant, obtained the knowledge which they had of their acceptance in his sight through the sacrifice which they offered unto him; and through the knowledge thus obtained their faith became sufficiently strong to lay hold upon the promise of eternal life, and to endure as seeing him who is invisible; and were enabled, through faith, to combat the powers of darkness, contend against the wiles of the adversary, overcome the world, and obtain the end of their faith, even the salvation of their souls.[6]

Till now, we have not said anything about charity, though faith, hope, and charity are clearly interwoven, interdependent concepts. (See 1 Cor. 13; Moro. 7:44–48.) We can understand the interrelationship of faith and hope fairly clearly through the paradigm, but where does charity enter in? As I have pondered this, I find a profoundly moving answer—charity enters in at every level, every aspect, every point. The pure love of Christ validates every level of action to make it productive. This seems to be what Paul meant when he said that one can prophesy or give alms or do numerous other things, yet such actions are meaningless if not done because of a love for God and fellowman. Charity is what lights our hope, strengthens our will, deepens our confirmation. It suffers long, endures much, is properly motivated, hopes for all things, and endures all things. I have not shown charity in the paradigm because it would need to be shown everywhere, for it permeates the whole process of faith and salvation. Mormon explained it thus:

> Charity is the pure love of Christ, and it endureth forever; and whoso is found possessed of it at the last day, it shall be well with him. Wherefore, my beloved brethren, pray unto the Father with all the energy of heart, that ye may be filled with this love, which he hath bestowed upon all who are true followers of his Son, Jesus Christ; that ye may become the sons of God; that when he shall appear we shall be like him, for we shall see him as he is; that we may have this hope; that we may be purified even as he is pure. (Moro. 7:47–48.)

Chapter 12

"Then Is His Grace Sufficient for You"

(Moroni 10:32)

When the Apostle Paul was imprisoned at Philippi, a distressed jailer asked him, "What must I do to be saved?" Without referring to obedience or repentance or good works, which he himself had so often spoken of, Paul simply answered, "Believe on the Lord Jesus Christ, and thou shalt be saved." (Acts 16:30–31.)

But in a church that also has many ancient and modern scriptural passages stressing works of righteousness and the importance of obedience to the laws and ordinances of the gospel, scriptural passages like Acts 16:31 often give rise to confusion. "As far as I'm concerned," one missionary said to his companion, "when somebody starts quoting Paul on salvation by grace, I just quote James on faith without works being dead [see James 2:17–26] and try to get off the subject as quickly as possible." Another time, a Sunday School teacher confessed to his class of teenagers, "Before I joined the Church, I quoted the words of Paul to everyone. Now I just kind of steer away from what he said. I know now how important good works are, so I put the emphasis there."

Paul's Defense of Salvation by Grace

Understanding these reactions isn't difficult. Paul's ringing defense of salvation by grace and his emphatic denunciation of justification through works of the law seem almost to run counter to our third Article of Faith: "We believe that through the Atonement of Christ, all mankind may be saved, by obedience to the laws and ordinances of the Gospel."

The problem in understanding Acts 16:31 isn't that Paul de-emphasized the atoning sacrifice of the Savior, but rather that he apparently de-emphasized the need for works. What missionary hasn't been confronted with Paul's statement to the saints in Rome: "If thou shalt confess with thy mouth the Lord Jesus, and shalt believe in thine heart that God hath raised him from the dead, thou shalt be saved." (Rom. 10:9.) Furthermore, in both Galatians and Romans, he pointedly rejected any idea that justification comes through works of the old law: "Knowing that a man is not justified by the works of the law, but by the faith of Jesus Christ, even we have believed in Jesus Christ, that we might be justified by the faith of Christ, and not by the works of the law: for by the works of the law shall no flesh be justified." (Gal. 2:16; see also Rom. 3:20, 28.)

Did Paul indeed reject the value of works for the disciple of Christ? Or was he simply reacting to the Jewish Christians who insisted that adherence to the law of Moses was necessary if one were to be saved? And, for us in the latter-days, does Paul's theological position coincide with that revealed in latter-day scripture?

Church members typically seek to synthesize Paul's teachings with Latter-day Saint theology in two different ways. The first suggests that by "the law" Paul meant only the law of Moses. Without a doubt, there is merit in this. Some Jewish Christians insisted that Christianity still required obedience to Mosaic principles like circumcision, the dietary laws, and the observance of certain festivals. Paul combatted that doctrine strongly, saying that no matter how strictly a person kept the law of Moses, it of itself would not bring salvation. The power of salvation comes only through Christ because of his atonement.

However, to limit Paul's meaning to the law of Moses alone would not be quite accurate. Paul rejected the adequacy of the Mosaic code in and of itself for salvation, but he made it broader than that too. For example, in warning the Ephesians about concluding that a man is saved by works, he makes no reference to the law: "For by grace are ye saved through faith; and that not of yourselves: it is the gift of God: not of works, lest any man should boast." (Eph. 2:8–9.) So while this explanation is somewhat correct, it does not go far enough.

The second typical explanation tries to divide the effects of the Atonement between physical death and spiritual death. According to this theory, the resurrection saves all from physical death—it is salvation by grace and is not dependent on anything we do. However, if we wish to overcome spiritual death and enter back into God's presence, we must be obedient to laws and principles. This is *exaltation by works.* Thus, according to this explanation, we are *saved* by grace and *exalted* by works.

This argument, however, has some fallacies, as discussed more fully in the section "Redemption Cometh in and through the Holy Messiah," chapter eight, pages 90–93. The most obvious fallacy is the assumption that *salvation* and *exaltation* mean different things. While the resurrection of the dead is certainly an integral part of the plan of salvation, and it is unconditional and independent of men's works, the term *salvation,* as used in the scriptures, does not mean physical resurrection alone. As Elder Bruce R. McConkie has pointed out, salvation is usually *synonymous* with exaltation: "*Salvation* in its true and full meaning is synonymous with *exaltation* or *eternal life* and consists in gaining an inheritance in the highest of the three heavens within the celestial kingdom. With few exceptions this is the salvation of which the scriptures speak. It is the salvation which the saints seek."[1]

Those who are uncomfortable with Paul's statements about grace and salvation should bear in mind that the same teachings are found in other scripture as well. Nephi, for example, nearly echoes Paul's words to the Ephesians when he says, "For we know that it is by grace that we are saved, after all we can do." (2 Ne. 25:23.) And Lehi's explanation of the Atonement to Jacob is remarkably similar to Paul's explanation of justification by faith in Romans 3, even down to the phrase "by the law no flesh is justified." (2 Ne. 2:5.) Likewise, Doctrine and Covenants 20:30–31 points out that both justification and sanctification come by grace.

Sin, Transgression, and the Law of Justice

How, then, are the principles of grace and works to be understood in relationship to each other? To come to that understanding, we must first look at some related concepts: the concepts of sin and transgression, of justice, and of the Fall. The concept of sin, first of all, rests upon the concept of law. If there were no law, there could be no sin (see 2 Ne. 2:13; Alma 42:17), because "sin is the transgression of the law" (1 Jn. 3:4). However, for purposes of understanding the Atonement better, drawing a distinction between two important variations in how the law may be violated might be helpful.

A person may violate the law in spite of his knowledge of it; that is, he breaks the law deliberately. But others may violate the law because they are unaware of its existence (ignorance) or because they do not have sufficient maturity to understand the implications of disobedience (lack of accountability). For clarification, let us use two terms to delineate the important differences in breaking the law. Any violation of the law that is willful and knowing, we shall call "sin." But any violation that results either from ignorance or lack of accountability, we shall call "transgression." The scriptures do not distinguish between these two terms consistently, but such a distinction may help us understand some important points about the Atonement.

For example, it helps us understand why children under the age of accountability cannot sin. (See D&C 29:47.) Any parents who have observed their children's behavior know that they often violate laws of the gospel. They hit brothers and sisters, demonstrate extreme selfishness at times, and can be unmercifully cruel to playmates. But while these are "transgressions," they are not "sins," because as Mormon points out, children are "not capable of committing sin." (See Moro. 8:8.) Much the same is true of those who have reached adulthood but have had relatively little or no opportunity to learn the principles of righteousness. They also violate the laws of God, sometimes horribly so, as in the case of many primitive peoples, but they are of necessity judged differently because they do not "sin" in the sense of rebelling willingly and deliberately against God.[2] (See Rom. 2:12; D&C 82:3.)

Standing alongside the concepts of sin and transgression is the law of justice, which implies consistency in reward and punishment. In other words, there would be no justice if one person could violate the law and escape its punishment while another was punished for the same act. Elder McConkie points out that "justice demands that a penalty be paid for every violation of the Lord's laws."[3] The opposite, or positive side, of that idea is that there is a reward for keeping the Lord's laws. (See D&C 130:20–21.) If punishments and rewards were not consistent throughout the universe and in all of eternity, justice would be violated. Briefly stated, then, the law of justice is that every violation of a law entails a punishment (ultimately suffering and misery) and every obedience of a law entails a reward (ultimately joy and peace).

Also embodied in the concept of justice is the idea that men are punished only for those things they themselves are guilty of. This would make it unjust to punish one man for another's sin; likewise, if through ignorance or lack of accountability, there is no guilt, meting out punishment would be unjust.

Having discussed sin, transgression, and justice, we have enough groundwork to better understand some of the important aspects of the atoning sacrifice of the Savior. One important application of the Atonement is to the fall of Adam. We know that it would be unjust for a person to be punished for violations he did not commit. Thus, all mankind being punished for Adam and Eve's disobedience would be unjust—it would be contrary to the law of justice. So regardless of the kinds of lives individuals have led, the effects of the fall of Adam—physical and spiritual death (i.e., the separation from God's presence)—are overcome for all souls who come to earth. Because of the Atonement, everyone will be resurrected and overcome physical death; and through the power of Christ, all will be brought back into the presence of God for the period of judgment and the assignment of glory. (See 1 Cor. 15:22; 2 Ne. 9:38.) Thus both physical death and that spiritual death resulting from Adam's fall are therefore removed through Christ.

However, *remaining* in the presence of God is a different, though related, matter. First, there is the case of those who are guilty of transgression but not of sin (in the sense we defined these terms). Where there is no knowledge or accountability, meting out punishment would be unjust. Nevertheless, justice demands payment for *every* violation of the law, whether the violation be sin or transgression. So the atonement of Christ automatically redeems children who die before they reach the age of accountability, and they are brought back into the presence of God. (See D&C 137:10.) Also, Jesus suffered the penalties of the law for those who violated the law without knowing it: "Where there is no law given there is no punishment; and where there is no punishment there is no condemnation; and where there is no condemnation the mercies of the Holy One of Israel have claim upon them, because of the atonement; for they are delivered by the power of him. For the atonement satisfieth the demands of his justice upon all those who have not the law given to them." (2 Ne. 9:25–26.)

Second, there is the case of those who sin knowingly, which is the case for all who reach the age of accountability. (See Rom. 3:23.) Though the Atonement has removed the effects of Adam's fall, our own personal falls will create another form of spiritual death. This is separation from God because of our own uncleanness and not because of Adam's fall. In other words, when we sin we become alienated from God. Our separation in this case is the result of our own actions.

The Doctrine and Covenants clearly points out that we could enter back into God's presence in this life if we would but purify ourselves from sin. (See D&C 67:10; 88:68; 93:1; see also Ether 3:13.) This purification from sin strongly involves the role of faith and works: faith leading to works of repentance and obedience is indispensable to the achievement of such a high and holy privilege. Even so, is it really by *our* works that we are saved from spiritual death? Again, Paul and the other prophets indicate no. And to understand this, we must once again look at the law of justice.

Remembering that every violation of the law brings punishment or suffering, there are only two ways possible to meet the demands of the law of justice. Either one keeps the law perfectly and never gets in debt to the law, or else one must pay the debt of suffering. The law is very exact. Even if it is violated only once, the violator is in its debt and must suffer the consequences. Perhaps this is why James wrote, "For whosoever shall keep the whole law, and yet offend in one point, he is guilty of all." (James 2:10.) We can see why both Paul and Lehi warned us that no one can be justified by the law: no one (with one exception) has ever kept the law perfectly. Every soul is in debt to the law, "for all have sinned, and come short of the glory of God." (Rom. 3:23.)

The Need for Grace

In Greek, the word translated as *grace* in the New Testament means "good-will, loving kindness, favor." It implies "the idea of kindness which bestows upon one what he has not deserved."[4] In the scriptural sense of the term, for a man to be justified (brought back into a proper relationship with God) by his own works is impossible, because no one keeps the law perfectly.

This was the very mistake that the Pharisees fell into with regard to the Mosaic law. We sometimes smile at their tremendously careful attempts to define the law and what was acceptable to it; but if a person holds that individuals are brought into the proper relationship with God by their works alone, then that person's position is similar to the Pharisees' view. If the tiniest infraction of the law puts one's relationship to God in jeopardy, then one must be extremely careful about any violation. The early rabbis simply carried that idea to its extreme.

For example, the law said, "Keep the Sabbath day holy." Very well then, what does that mean in terms of my behavior? Well, for one thing, I mustn't do any work. All right, but what exactly could be considered as work? Gardening? Cleaning the house? Could I rearrange the furniture? What happens, for instance, if my house should catch fire on the Sabbath? Is it "work" to take things out and save them from destruction? Are these ridiculous questions? Not if you're seeking justification by the law. And so, with great precision, the rabbis enumerated what could and could not be saved if a person's house were endangered by fire on the Sabbath. They even defined how much food could be saved, depending on what time of day the fire occurred. If it broke out on Friday evening (the Jewish Sabbath went from sundown Friday to sundown Saturday), one could save enough for three meals; if Saturday morning, two meals; and if Saturday afternoon, only one.[5] These are the kinds of logical conclusions we are forced to make if we seek justification by the works of the law alone.

To better see why such attempts are ineffective, let us analyze a parable given by Elder Boyd K. Packer, in which he refers to the spiritual jeopardy of all those who are born on this earth:

> There once was a man who wanted something very much. It seemed more important than anything else in his life. In order for him to have his desire, he incurred a great debt.
>
> He had been warned about going into that much debt, and particularly about his creditor. But it seemed so important for him to do what he wanted to do and to have what he wanted right now. He was sure he could pay for it later.
>
> So he signed a contract. He would pay it off some time along the way. He didn't worry too much about it, for the due date seemed such a long time away.[6]

Thus, having entered mortality in a state of innocence, people begin to sin and lose their perfect worthiness. They incur a debt (a burden of sin), which, unless paid in full, will extend into the eternities—"the spiritual death, which is separation from the presence of our Heavenly Father."[7] Under these circumstances (disregarding the Atonement for the moment), even if they suddenly realized that they had cheated themselves of the opportunity to go back to God's presence and had stopped increasing their debts (that is, they stopped committing sin and became obedient), there is still no way that they could ever qualify to return to the Father. Even if they committed only one sin (which is unrealistic, of course, for we sin many times), they still could not get back.

Full payment is the condition for admittance, and no exceptions can exist—justice is perfectly exact. Ceasing to sin merely stops the increase in the burden of debt—it does not generate the means to repay. There is, of course, an advantage in keeping the burden of sin (the debt to the law) as small as possible; nevertheless, at the commission of the first sin, a person loses his ability to return to God. Elder Packer continues: "As it always does, the day came, and the contract fell due. The debt had not been fully paid. His creditor appeared and demanded payment in full." The debtor's dilemma was acute:

> "I cannot pay you, for I have not the power to do so," he confessed.
>
> "Then," said the creditor, "we will exercise the contract, take your possessions, and you shall go to prison. . . . "
>
> "Can you not extend the time or forgive the debt?" the debtor begged. . . . "Will you not show mercy?"
>
> The creditor replied, "Mercy is always so one-sided. It would serve only you. If I show mercy to you, it will leave me unpaid. . . . Mercy cannot rob justice."
>
> There they were: One meting out justice, the other pleading for mercy. Neither could prevail except at the expense of the other. . . .
>
> Both laws, it seemed, could not be served. They are two eternal ideals that appear to contradict one another. Is there no way for justice to be fully served, and mercy also?

> There is a way! . . . But it takes someone else. And so it happened this time.
>
> The debtor had a friend. He came to help. He knew the debtor well. . . . He wanted to help because he loved him. He stepped between them, faced the creditor, and made his offer.
>
> "I will pay the debt. . . . You demanded justice. Though he cannot pay you, I will do so. You will have been justly dealt with and can ask no more. . . . "
>
> And so it was that the creditor was paid in full. . . . The debtor, in turn, had been extended mercy. Both laws stood fulfilled. Because there was a mediator, justice had claimed its full share, and mercy was fully satisfied.[8]

Once the debt was established, then, outside payment had to be introduced from somewhere or our debts would have stood forever. Thus it is that only in the sacrifice of the Only Begotten Son, who had no sin, could we be delivered from this sad state.

Christ—the Source of Unlimited Reserves

The Savior could effect our deliverance for two important reasons. First, he met the demands of the law of justice for himself because *he kept the laws of God perfectly*. In other words, Christ was justified by his works. He avoided the debt altogether and qualified himself to return to the Father—the only one of all mankind to do so. Second, he met the demands of the law for all of the rest of mankind. He himself owed no debt to the law, but he went before it and in essence said: "I am perfect and therefore owe you no suffering. However, I will pay the debt for all mankind. I will undergo suffering that I might pay the price for every transgression and sin ever committed by any man."

In the Garden of Gethsemane and on the cross, Christ paid the price by suffering for every sin as though he himself had committed them, satisfying fully the law of justice. Such suffering is beyond the power of any mortal man to endure. We can't understand how he did it, only that he did and that "through Him mercy can be fully extended to each of us without offending the eternal law of justice."[9] In terms of Elder Packer's parable, he generated sufficient payment to satisfy the debt of every other man. He met the demands of the law for himself through obedience and for all others through suffering.

Alma told his son Corianton that mercy could not rob justice, or else "God would cease to be God." (Alma 42:25.) That is the case with the merciful love of the Father and the Son. In fact, mercy paid justice! Their Love said to Justice, by virtue of the price paid in the Garden, "Here is payment for the wrongs committed. You are paid in full. Now let the captives go free."

In one of the most beautiful images in all of scripture, we find the solution to that awful dilemma we all face as sinners. We are standing before the bar as defendants, facing the great judge, God the Father. Our "Advocate with the Father" steps forward, not to refute the charges or to hold up a record of our good works to counterbalance our guilt, but to plead our case in a different manner:

> Listen to him who is the advocate with the Father, who is pleading your cause before him—saying: Father, behold the sufferings and death of him who did no sin, in whom thou wast well pleased; behold the blood of thy Son which was shed, the blood of him whom thou gavest that thyself might be glorified; wherefore, Father, spare these my brethren that believe on my name, that they may come unto me and have everlasting life. (D&C 45:3–5.)

Nothing man could do for himself could bring him past the judgment bar successfully without such an Advocate. That is why eternal life is always a gift, and those who receive it do so by "inheritance." It is interesting to note that the word *inherit* and its cognate words are used seventy-eight times in the Doctrine and Covenants, while the word *earned* and its related words are not used once.

What Must We Do?

The sacrifice that pays the debt and frees us from the results of our own spiritual death, though it comes to us through the grace and goodness of God, does not mean we do nothing. What, then, are we to do if Jesus Christ has done so much for us? Here are the steps: they are first, have faith in the Lord Jesus Christ, then repent, then be baptized for the remission of sins. If we truly move through those steps—mentally, spiritually, and physically—then we are prepared for the reception of the Holy Ghost. When we are given the *gift* (there's that word again) of the Holy Ghost, we have overcome spiritual death to a degree, for we have come into the presence of one member of the Godhead. The Holy Ghosts's role, of course, is to help purify, guide, teach, and strengthen us so that we can fully overcome spiritual death by coming back into the presence of the Father and the Son—another way of saying that his role is to help us endure to the end.

Now with all this in mind, remember that Paul said we are justified *by* faith (see Gal. 2:16; Rom. 3:28), which is the first principle of the gospel. In other words, faith is the principle that activates the power of the Atonement in our lives, and we are put back into a proper relationship with God (justification) as faith activates that power. There are marvelous implications in this concept, and perhaps another analogy can help us see more clearly the role faith and works have in relationship to salvation:

Each of us is like a powerhouse on a mighty river. The powerhouse has no power residing in itself; the potential power rests in the energy of the river. When that source of power flows through the generators of the power plant, power is transferred from the river to the power plant and sent out into the homes (lives) of others. The atonement of Christ is the power in the river. Faith is the generators that can harness that power. The power to achieve justification does not reside in us. We require the power of the atonement of Christ flowing into us. If no power is being generated, we do not—indeed, cannot—turn the generators by hand (justification by works); but rather, we make an effort to remove those things that have blocked the power from flowing into the generators (working righteousness as a result of faith).

With this analogy, we can more clearly understand why the scriptures stress that faith *includes* works. (See James 2:17–26.) Righteous works in themselves do not save us because none of us can work perfectly enough to earn salvation. The atoning power of God saves us. Obedience, commitment, and repentance—these are the works of faith that open up the channels so that the power of the atoning sacrifice of Christ can flow into us, redeem us from sin, and bring us back into the presence of God. Disobedience and wickedness dam those channels. (How literal is the word *damnation!*) Thus, each of us determines whether we will be able to seek the gift and power of the Atonement in our behalf.

There is no need to go to extraordinary lengths to apologize for Paul or try to explain away his statements on salvation by grace. We *are* saved by grace—saved by Christ's love from physical and spiritual death; saved by Christ's love from Adam's fall and our own; saved from sin and transgression by the grace or gifts of God. The atoning power of God unto salvation is a freely available gift from him—but our works of righteousness, welling up from fountains of faith, are essential to bring the gift into power in our lives. Sin brings alienation from God. The more we sin, the greater the alienation and the more difficult it becomes to effectively tap the power of God, which alone is sufficient to save us from our sins.

President Joseph Fielding Smith has summarized the relationship between grace and works as follows:

> So Paul taught these people—who thought that they could be saved by some power that was within them, or by observing the law of Moses—he pointed out to them the fact that if it were not for the mission of Jesus Christ, if it were not for this great atoning sacrifice, they could not be redeemed. And therefore it was by the grace of God that they are saved, not by any work on their part, for they were absolutely helpless. Paul was absolutely right.
>
> And on the other hand, James taught just as the Lord taught, just as Paul had taught in other scripture, that it is our duty, of necessity, to labor, to strive in diligence, and faith, keeping the commandments of the Lord, if we would obtain that inheritance which is promised to the faithful. . . .
>
> So it is easy to understand that we must accept the mission of Jesus Christ. We must believe that it is through his grace that we are saved, that he performed for us that labor which we were unable to perform for ourselves, and did for us those things which were essential to our salvation, which were beyond our power; and also that we are under the commandment and the necessity of performing the labors that are required of us as set forth in the commandments known as the gospel of Jesus Christ.[10]

Thus, we can with Paul fervently exclaim that "the wages of sin is death; but the gift of God is eternal life through Jesus Christ our Lord." (Rom. 6:23.) We should continue to stress the importance of faith, of repentance, of obedience and strive with all our hearts to be full of faith and demonstrate good works in our lives. But we should never lose sight of the great overriding fact of the grace of our Lord and Savior and the wholly *central* part it plays in our atonement and salvation.

Moroni, in the closing words of the Book of Mormon,

teaches the relationship between the grace of Christ and the need for our righteous efforts. Note how he keeps distinctly clear what it is that perfects us, and yet what must happen in our lives to bring that about.

> Come unto Christ, and be perfected in him, and deny yourselves of all ungodliness; and if ye shall deny yourselves of all ungodliness, and love God with all your might, mind and strength, then is his grace sufficient for you, that by his grace ye may be perfect in Christ; and if by the grace of God ye are perfect in Christ, ye can in nowise deny the power of God.
>
> And again, if ye by the grace of God are perfect in Christ, and deny not his power, then are ye sanctified in Christ by the grace of God, through the shedding of the blood of Christ, which is in the covenant of the Father unto the remission of your sins, that ye become holy, without spot. (Moro. 10:32–33.)

Chapter 13

"I Would That Ye Should Be Perfect Even As I"

(3 Nephi 12:48)

The Savior has given us a commandment, recorded twice in scripture, to be perfect, even as he or his Father in heaven is perfect. (See Matt. 5:48; 3 Ne. 12:48; see also 3 Ne. 27:27.) Jesus Christ not only has personally offered himself as a savior to fulfill the plan of salvation, but also has been set as a high standard for us to reach. In some way, this latter facet of the Savior's mission is integral to the plan of salvation too. The purpose of the plan of redemption is to bring us exaltation, and the work and sacrifice of the Savior are to lift us past the obstacles to that goal. As the Lord told the Saints, "ye are not able to abide the presence of God now, neither the ministering of angels; wherefore, continue in patience until ye are perfected." (D&C 67:13.)

Being Perfected

Many of us have wondered whether the commandment means we have to be perfect in order to achieve exaltation. Whether we answer this question yes or no depends on how we define the word *perfect*. One definition of *perfect* is "never having flaw or error." In this sense, only one person in all of human history—our Savior—has been perfect. Not once in all his mortal life—not as a child, not as an adult—was he out of harmony with the Father's will. In this sense, we clearly do *not* have to be perfect to be saved. Otherwise, there would be no hope for any of us, for as Paul said, "All have sinned, and come short of the glory of God." (Rom. 3:23.)

But *perfect* can also mean "having all flaws and errors removed." Perhaps a clearer question to ask ourselves is "Do we have to be *perfected* to be exalted?" Here the scriptural answer is a resounding yes. In numerous references, the Lord says that no unclean thing can dwell in his presence. (See 1 Ne. 10:21; Alma 7:21; 3 Ne. 27:19; Moses 6:57.) Obviously, then, we must repent of those flaws identified as sins and become clean before we can be exalted. But what of other flaws—those that don't qualify as sins but are nevertheless imperfections?

The Prophet Joseph Smith said that our very faith rests in knowing that the attributes of God, such as his love, mercy, power, and knowledge, are all held in perfection.[1] An imperfect God would indeed be a contradiction in terms. At some point, then, if we are to become like God, we must be perfect, without any flaw or error. But must we achieve that state in this life? Here the prophets have spoken plainly. In the great sermon known as the King Follett discourse, the Prophet Joseph taught:

> When you climb up a ladder, you must begin at the bottom, and ascend step by step, until you arrive at the top; and so it is with the principles of the Gospel—you must begin with the first and go on until you learn all the principles of exaltation. But *it will be a great while after you have passed through the veil before you will have learned them. It is not all to be comprehended in this world; it will be a great work to learn our salvation and exaltation even beyond the grave.*[2]

President Joseph F. Smith confirmed this idea:

> We do not look for absolute perfection in man. *Mortal man is not capable of being absolutely perfect.* Nevertheless, it is given to us to be as perfect in the sphere in which we are called to be and to act, as it is for the Father in heaven to be pure and righteous in the more exalted sphere in which he acts. We will find in the scriptures the words of the Savior himself to his disciples, in which he required that they should be perfect, even as their Father in heaven is perfect; that they should be righteous, even as he is righteous. I do not expect that we can be as perfect as Christ, that we can be as righteous as God. But I believe that we can strive for that perfection with the intelligence that we possess, and the knowledge that we have of the principles of life and salvation.[3]

Elder Joseph Fielding Smith spoke with equal clarity on the same subject:

> Salvation does not come all at once; we are commanded to be perfect even as our Father in heaven is perfect. *It will take us ages to accomplish this end, for there will be greater progress beyond the grave,* and it will be there that the faithful will overcome all things, and receive all things, even the fulness of the Father's glory. I believe the Lord meant just what he said: that we should be perfect, as our Father in heaven is perfect. That will not come all at once, but line upon line, and precept upon precept, example upon example, and even then not as long as we live in this mortal life, for *we will have to go even beyond the grave before we reach that perfection and shall be like God.*
>
> But here we lay the foundation.[4]

While these statements clarify that full perfection is not achievable in mortality, each also suggests that we should always strive for perfection in our lives. Perfection is our eternal goal; it is what we must eventually achieve if we are to become like our Father. A primary purpose of mortality is to come as close to perfection as possible before we die.

Is Perfection a Practical Goal?

The idea of achieving perfection, wonderful as it may be, seems staggering. How many of us have also wondered how to keep perfection as a goal without becoming so discouraged or depressed with our failings that we lose hope and give up trying to perfect ourselves? I would like to suggest eight practical ideas that can help us maintain the balance between eternal goals and mortal realities.

1. Remember that one of Satan's strategies, especially with good people, is to whisper in their ears: "If you are not perfect, you are failing." This is one of his most effective deceptions, for it contains some elements of truth. But it *is* deception nonetheless. While we should never be completely satisfied until we *are* perfect, we should recognize that God is pleased with every effort we make—no matter how faltering—to better ourselves. One of the most commonly listed attributes of God is that he is long-suffering and quick to show mercy. He wants us to strive for perfection, but the fact that we have not yet achieved it does not mean we are failing.

2. Feelings of failure are natural and common to most people. Elder Neal A. Maxwell put it this way:

> I speak, not to the slackers in the Kingdom, but to those who carry their own load and more; not to those lulled into false security, but to those buffeted by false insecurity, who, though laboring devotedly in the Kingdom, have recurring feelings of falling forever short. . . .
>
> The first thing to be said of this feeling of inadequacy is that it is normal. . . . Following celestial road signs while in telestial traffic jams is not easy, especially when we are not just moving next door—or even across town.[5]

Even such great men as Moses, Enoch, and Gideon were reluctant to believe that they were capable of doing what God called them to do. To their credit, they tried anyway—and, with the Lord's help, succeeded. (See Ex. 4:10; Moses 6:31; Judg. 6:15.)

3. The Lord himself has warned us about being unrealistic in our expectations. To a young prophet, deeply contrite over losing 116 pages of sacred manuscript, the Lord said: "Do not run faster or labor more than you have strength." (D&C 10:4.) And after a lengthy and powerful call to repentance, King Benjamin gave this counsel: "See that all these things are done in wisdom and order; for it is not requisite that a man should run faster than he has strength. And again, it is expedient that he should be diligent, that thereby he might win the prize; therefore, all things must be done in order." (Mosiah 4:27.)

4. Remember that the scriptures are replete with examples of great men and women who moved toward perfection *through missteps, in spite of failings,* and *having to overcome* their weaknesses. For example, the author of the second Gospel is the same Mark who earlier had left his missionary service, deserting Paul and Barnabus. (See Acts 12:25; 13:13; 15:37–38.) The same Corianton who was severely chastized for being immoral on his mission (see Alma 39:3–5, 11) was later listed among the faithful who helped bring peace to the Nephites (see Alma 49:30). Finally, the people of Melchizedek at one point had "waxed strong in iniquity and abomination; yea, they had all gone astray; they were full of all manner of wickedness." But "they did repent" and went to join the city of Enoch. (Alma 13:17–18; see JST Gen. 14:34.)

5. The Lord not only looks at our works, he also takes into account the desires of our hearts. (See Alma 41:3; D&C 88:109; 137:9.) This means that even if we don't always perfectly translate our good desires into action, these desires will be included in our final evaluation. Elder Bruce R. McConkie described what it takes to be saved:

> What we do in this life is chart a course leading to eternal

> life. That course begins here and now and continues in the realms ahead. We must determine in our hearts and in our souls, with all the power and ability we have, that from this time forward we will press on in righteousness; by so doing we can go where God and Christ are. *If we make that firm determination, and are in the course of our duty when this life is over, we will continue in that course in eternity.* That same spirit that possesses our bodies at the time we depart from this mortal life will have power to possess our bodies in the eternal world. *If we go out of this life loving the Lord, desiring righteousness, and seeking to acquire the attributes of godliness, we will have that same spirit in the eternal world,* and we will then continue to advance and progress until an ultimate, destined day when we will possess, receive, and inherit all things.[6]

6. "Hanging in there," in modern vernacular, is one of the most important keys to becoming perfected. This is what the scriptures mean by enduring to the end. Some people live out years of righteousness and then, when life takes a downward turn or becomes boring, tedious, and monotonous, they become discouraged and decide that striving for perfection is no longer worth their effort. After a remarkable life of faith and commitment, King David lost his exaltation because he did not continue in his set course.

Somehow, some of us get it into our heads that, if we are not making great, dramatic leaps forward spiritually, we are not progressing. Actually, for most of us, the challenge of living the gospel is that progress comes in almost imperceptible increments. Very seldom can we look back over one day and see great progress. Becoming like God takes years and years of striving, and trying again.

We must also keep in mind that just because we are striving to better ourselves does not mean all problems, challenges, and setbacks will disappear. Elder Gordon B. Hinckley, quoting columnist Jenkins Lloyd Jones, reminded us that life will always have its challenges:

> Anyone who imagines that bliss is normal is going to waste a lot of time running around shouting that he's been robbed. The fact is that most putts don't drop, most beef is tough, most children grow up to be just people, most successful marriages require a high degree of mutual toleration, most jobs are more often dull than otherwise. Life is like an old time rail journey . . . delays, sidetracks, smoke, dust, cinders, and jolts, interspersed only occasionally by beautiful vistas and thrilling bursts of speed. The trick is to thank the Lord for letting you have the ride.[7]

7. To overcome the discouragement we feel as we see our failings and imperfections, we should remember that we learn and progress in spiritual things much the same way we learn and progress in physical things. Parents are not disappointed when their baby first learns to crawl before he walks. It is the natural order of things. Likewise, no one expects a student to understand calculus until he has first learned the numbers, then the laws of addition and subtraction, and then the mysteries of algebra and trigonometry. President Spencer W. Kimball noted that "working toward perfection is not a one-time decision but a process to be pursued throughout one's lifetime."[8] So why is it that we demand instant perfection? Why should we expect to run spiritual four-minute miles until we have jogged hundreds upon hundreds of times around the spiritual tracks of our lives? Why do we expect to work spiritual calculus before we have mastered the spiritual multiplication tables? And why should we be disappointed when we cannot play spiritual symphonies if we have not yet taught ourselves to play the spiritual scales?

8. Finally and most important, perfection is not left up to us alone. Along the way, the Lord has given us innumerable helps: the ordinances of salvation, the organizations of the Church, the priesthood, the guidance and gifts of the Holy Ghost, repentance and forgiveness, temples, scriptures,

home teaching and visiting teaching. The list goes on and on and includes everything the gospel and the Church have to offer.

Even with all this, however, the key to perfection is the Savior himself. If at times we feel weary or think that we can't do enough or do it well enough to be perfected, we have lost sight of the Atonement. We are in a mindset where we think we are supposed to make gods of ourselves. Stated that way, of course, the notion is foolish, but we must remember that Jesus Christ, because of his atoning sacrifice and his power, is the one who makes godhood—and glorification, sanctification, perfection, and everything else that goes with it—possible for us. His is the power behind our quest for perfection. So, though the goal may at times seem intimidating and the work overwhelming, he can say to us, "Come unto me, all ye that labour and are heavy laden, and I will give you rest. Take my yoke upon you, and learn of me; for I am meek and lowly in heart: and ye shall find rest unto your souls. For my yoke is easy, and my burden is light." (Matt. 11:28–30.) Remember, the burden of perfecting ourselves is his burden too; and since he is carrying it with us and for us, it is light enough for us to carry.

Perfection is our goal. But let us not be thrown off course when we do not fully achieve it in this life. And most of all, let us, as we strive for that lofty goal, remember the Lord's promise to those of us who so keenly sense our weaknesses and inadequacies: "If men come unto me I will show unto them their weakness. I give unto men weakness that they may be humble; and my grace is sufficient for all men that humble themselves before me; for if they humble themselves before me, and have faith in me, then will I make weak things become strong unto them." (Ether 12:27.)

Notes

Chapter 2

1. Alfred Edersheim, *Sketches of Jewish Social Life in the Days of Christ* (Grand Rapids, Michigan: Wm. B. Eerdmans Publishing Company, 1979), 70.

2. *Smith's Historical Geography,* as cited in Merrill F. Unger, ed., *Unger's Bible Dictionary,* 3d ed. (Chicago: Moody Press, 1966), 779.

3. See Edersheim, 105.

4. See ibid., 143–44.

5. See Robert Young, *Analytical Concordance to the Bible* (Grand Rapids: Wm. B. Eerdmans, 1972), 647.

6. From D&C 20:1 we learn that the birth date of the Savior was April 6. See also James E. Talmage, *Jesus the Christ,* Classics in Mormon Literature Edition (Salt Lake City: Deseret Book, 1982), 96–98 (102–4 earlier editions). Counting nine months backwards puts the time somewhere around July.

7. In Luke 2:24, we are told that Mary and Joseph offered as the required sacrifice for their firstborn son two turtledoves or pigeons. In Leviticus 12:6–8, where the requirement is given, we are told that the sacrifice should be a lamb, but if the family "be not able" (that is, they are financially unable to afford a lamb), they may instead offer the turtledoves or pigeons.

8. See Unger, 40.

9. See note six above.

10. Josephus, *The Antiquities of the Jews,* XVII, ix, 3, in *Josephus: Complete Works,* tr. William Whiston (Grand Rapids: Kregel Publications, 1960).

11. See Josephus, *Wars of the Jews,* VI, ix, 3, in *Complete Works.*

12. Unger, 527.

13. Harold B. Lee, "I Walked Today Where Jesus Walked," *BYU Speeches of the Year,* December 10, 1958, p. 5.

14. M. R. Vincent, *Word Studies in the New Testament* (MacDill AFB, Florida: MacDonald Publishing Company, n.d.), 142.

15. See Unger, 195.

Chapter 3

1. The King James Version of the Isaiah passage has some different wording from the KJV in Luke 4, but the meaning is essentially the same. Some translations of Isaiah have wordings that are closer to the passage in Luke.

KJV Isaiah 61:1–2: "The Spirit of the Lord God is upon me; because the Lord [the *he* in Luke 4:18] hath anointed me to preach good tidings [same as *gospel*] unto the meek [sometimes translated *poor*]; he hath sent me to bind up [referring to wrapping wounds, thus similar to *heal*] the brokenhearted, to proclaim liberty [same as *preach deliverance*] to the captives, and the opening of the prison [parallel to *set at liberty*] to them that are bound [instead of *bruised*]; to proclaim the acceptable year of the Lord." Though this text leaves out entirely one phrase in the Savior's quote, "and recovering of sight to the blind," some translations include it instead of or in addition to "and the opening of the prison to them that are bound." The ancient Greek translation of the Hebrew Old Testament has the phrase. Remember that the text the Savior was reading from was much, much older than the texts from which the KJV was translated.

Chapter 4

1. H. Curtis Wright, *A Thing of Naught—World Judgment and the Trial of Jesus Christ* (Provo, Utah: Brigham Young University Extension Publications, 1960), 9; italics added.

2. For an excellent summary of the illegalities of the trial, see Talmage, 598–601 (644–48 earlier editions).

3. See Talmage, 620–21 (668–69 earlier editions).

4. "I Stand All Amazed," *Hymns of The Church of Jesus Christ of Latter-day Saints* (Salt Lake City: The Church of Jesus Christ of Latter-day Saints, 1985), no. 80.

5. James E. Talmage, "The Parable of the Grateful Cat," *Improvement Era,* August 1916, pp. 875–76.

6. Eric G. Anderson, "The Vertical Wilderness," *Private Practice,* November 1979, p. 17; italics added.

7. Cited in Wright, 35.

Chapter 5

1. Eusebius, *The Ecclesiastical History and the Martyrs of Palestine,* tr. Hugh Lawlor and John Oulton, 2 vols. (London: S.P.C.K., 1954), 1:II.23.
2. Josephus, *Antiquities,* XX, ix, 1.
3. Eusebius, 1:III.10–11 and III.32.1–4.
4. William Smith, *A Dictionary of the Bible* (Grand Rapids: Zondervan Publishing House, 1967 rev. ed.), *s.v.* Simon; F. N. Peloubet, *Peloubet's Bible Dictionary* (Grand Rapids: Zondervan, 1971), *s.v.* Simon.
5. See Stephen and Shirley Smith Ricks, "Jewish Religious Education in the Meridian of Time," *Ensign,* October 1987, pp. 60–62.

Chapter 6

1. Bruce R. McConkie, *The Promised Messiah: The First Coming of Christ* (Salt Lake City: Deseret Book, 1978), 453.
2. Andrew Jukes, *The Law of the Offerings* (Grand Rapids: Kregel, 1976 reprint ed.), 14–15.
3. Jukes, 44–45.
4. For a more detailed discussion of the typology of Old Testament sacrifices and ordinances, see Richard D. Draper, "Sacrifice and Offerings: An Ordinance Given by Jehovah to Reveal Himself as the Christ," in *A Symposium on the Old Testament* (Salt Lake City: Corporation of the President of The Church of Jesus Christ of Latter-day Saints, 1979), 71–78.
5. See D. Kelly Ogden, "A Sampler of Biblical Plants," *Ensign,* August 1990, pp. 37–38.
6. Joseph Fielding Smith, *Doctrines of Salvation,* comp. Bruce R. McConkie, 3 vols. (Salt Lake City: Bookcraft, 1954–56), 3:180; italics omitted.
7. McConkie, *Promised Messiah,* 431–32.
8. C. F. Keil and F. Delitzsch, "The Pentateuch, Three Volumes in One," in *Commentary on the Old Testament in Ten Volumes* (Grand Rapids: Eerdmans, 1973), 1 (The Third Book of Moses): 398.
9. McConkie, *Promised Messiah,* 432–33.
10. See Adam Clarke, *The Holy Bible . . . with Commentary and Critical Notes,* 6 vols. (New York: N. Bangs and J. Emory, for the Methodist Episcopal Church, 1827-31), 1:134; John 19:17.
11. Ibid., 1:146; italics added.
12. Keil and Delitzsch, 1 (The First Book of Moses): 253; italics added.

Chapter 8

1. James E. Talmage, *The Articles of Faith,* Classics in Mormon Literature Edition, with rev. pagination and typography (Salt Lake City: Deseret Book, 1984), 63 (70 earlier editions).

2. Bruce R. McConkie, *Mormon Doctrine,* 2nd ed. (Salt Lake City: Bookcraft, 1966), 65.

3. Marion G. Romney, "Jesus Christ, Lord of the Universe," *Improvement Era,* November 1968, p. 46.

4. Samuel Fallows, *The Popular and Critical Bible Encyclopedia and Scriptural Dictionary,* 3 vols. (Chicago: The Howard-Serverance Co., 1905–6), 2:1009.

5. *Bible Dictionary,* LDS Edition of the King James Version, *s.v.* Grace; italics added.

6. See Joseph Smith, *Lectures on Faith* (Salt Lake City: Deseret Book, 1985), 3:4.

7. Ibid., 5:1.

8. See Daniel H. Ludlow, "Question/Answer," *The New Era,* September 1973, p. 14.

9. See Talmage, *Articles of Faith,* 63–64 (70 earlier editions).

Chapter 9

1. Joseph Fielding Smith, comp., *Teachings of the Prophet Joseph Smith* (Salt Lake City: Deseret Book, 1938), 150–51.

Chapter 10

1. Henry B. Eyring, "Remembrance and Gratitude," *Ensign,* November 1989, pp. 12–13; italics added.

2. Thomas Y. Canby, "Reshaping Our Lives: Advanced Materials," *National Geographic,* December 1989, p. 781.

3. *Hymns,* no. 301.

4. Adam Clarke, "Matthew to the Acts," in *The New Testament of Our Lord and Savior Jesus Christ,* vol. 5 of *Clarke's Bible Commentary,* 6 vols. (Nashville: Abingdon Press, n.d.), 5:468; italics in original.

5. A careful reading of Mosiah 3 shows that all but verses one and two are a direct quote of the message delivered by the angel. That is also confirmed in Mosiah 4:1.

6. Ezra Taft Benson, "Beware of Pride," *Ensign,* May 1989, p. 4.

7. LDS Bible Dictionary, *s.v.* Grace; italics added.

8. Ezra Taft Benson, *God, Family, Country* (Salt Lake City: Deseret Book, 1974), 199.

Chapter 11

1. Smith, *Lectures on Faith,* 7:7.

2. Vaughn J. Featherstone, "As If They Would Ask Him to Tarry a

Little Longer," in *Speeches of the Year, 1975* (Provo: Brigham Young University Press, 1976), 375.

3. Smith, *Lectures on Faith,* 1:13–17.
4. Ibid., 3:2–5.
5. See Ibid., 6:7.
6. Ibid., 6:11.

Chapter 12

1. McConkie, *Mormon Doctrine,* 670.
2. Smith, *Teachings of Joseph Smith,* 218.
3. McConkie, *Mormon Doctrine,* 406.
4. *Greek-English Lexicon of the New Testament,* trans. Joseph Henry Thayer (Grand Rapids: Zondervan, 1962), *s.v. cháris* [grace].
5. See *Misknayoth* [The Oral Law], "Tractate Sabbath," 16:2.
6. Boyd K. Packer, "The Mediator," *Ensign,* May 1977, p. 54.
7. Ibid., p. 56.
8. Ibid., pp. 54–55.
9. Ibid., p. 56.
10. Smith, *Doctrines of Salvation,* 2:310–11.

Chapter 13

1. See Smith, *Lectures on Faith,* 4:1–19.
2. Smith, *Teachings of Joseph Smith,* 348; italics added.
3. Joseph F. Smith, *Gospel Doctrine,* 5th ed. (Salt Lake City, Deseret Book Co., 1939), 132; italics added.
4. Smith, *Doctrines of Salvation,* 2:18; italics added.
5. Neal A. Maxwell, "Notwithstanding My Weakness," *Ensign,* November 1976, p. 12.
6. Bruce R. McConkie, "The Seven Deadly Heresies," in *Speeches of the Year, 1980* (Provo: Brigham Young University, 1981), 78–79; italics added.
7. Gordon B. Hinckley, Address Given to Religious Educators, September 1978, p. 4.
8. Spencer W. Kimball, "Hold Fast to the Iron Rod," *Ensign,* November 1978, p. 6.

Scriptural References

Index